# Your Free Open Source Music Studio

G.W. Childs IV

**Course Technology PTR**
*A part of Cengage Learning*

COURSE TECHNOLOGY
CENGAGE Learning·

Australia • Brazil • Japan • Korea • Mexico • Singapore • Spain • United Kingdom • United States

# COURSE TECHNOLOGY
CENGAGE Learning™

**Your Free Open Source Music Studio**
G.W. Childs IV

Publisher and General Manager, Course Technology PTR: Stacy L. Hiquet

Associate Director of Marketing: Sarah Panella

Manager of Editorial Services: Heather Talbot

Marketing Manager: Mark Hughes

Acquisitions Editor: Orren Merton

Project Editor/Copy Editor: Cathleen D. Small

Interior Layout Tech: MPS Limited, a Macmillan Company

Cover Designer: Mike Tanamachi

Indexer: Kelly Talbot Editing Services

Proofreader: Kelly Talbot Editing Services

For product information and technology assistance, contact us at
**Cengage Learning Customer & Sales Support, 1-800-354-9706**

For permission to use material from this text or product, submit all requests online at **www.cengage.com/permissions**
Further permissions questions can be emailed to
**permissionrequest@cengage.com**

All trademarks are the property of their respective owners.

All images © Cengage Learning unless otherwise noted.

Library of Congress Control Number: 2011924486

ISBN-13: 978-1-4354-5836-9

ISBN-10: 1-4354-5836-2

**Course Technology, a part of Cengage Learning**
20 Channel Center Street
Boston, MA 02210
USA

Cengage Learning is a leading provider of customized learning solutions with office locations around the globe, including Singapore, the United Kingdom, Australia, Mexico, Brazil, and Japan. Locate your local office at: **international.cengage.com/region**

Cengage Learning products are represented in Canada by Nelson Education, Ltd.

For your lifelong learning solutions, visit **courseptr.com**

Visit our corporate website at **cengage.com**

Printed in the United States of America
1 2 3 4 5 6 7 13 12 11

*To Eddie Glen Briscoe,*

*You encouraged me in my pursuits every time we talked, but when I started writing, that's when you really made me believe I could—even when I didn't.*

*The next book I was writing was going to be dedicated to you. I wish you could've been here to see it. Then again, I guess you are. I miss you.*

# Preface

Let's zoom back to 2006. I was just beginning my first leap into the wonderful world of freelance sound design, music, and editing. As excited as I was, I was hardly financially ready for the expenses of the move I was making. However, ignorance often allows us to do things that we've never thought possible, right? You see, I'd become very comfortable with the amount of equipment, software, and so on that my former employer had outfitted me with, and with all of that gone, I could only incrementally discover what I was missing and needing as I went along.

At the beginning of this freelance journey, I was doing a lot of remixes for a label with whom I was not signed, but they did love my work, so I kept getting freelance jobs from them. Within my first week of working in an office funded entirely by me, I began to be aware of things that I was going to sorely miss. My Waves plug-ins were gone now, as were my wave editor (Sound Forge), my soundproof office, the friendly receptionist down the hall, another plug-in, another plug-in, MS Office...argh!

My head began to swim as I realized I was missing some of the tools I desperately needed for polish, creation, editing, and more. It was a sobering moment, because I had a small nest egg to live on that needed to stretch for an unforeseen amount of time, and purchasing package after package of software every time I realized I was missing something was going to add up.

For many people in my place, piracy becomes an alluring alternative. Why purchase when you can download for free? However, I'd just come from working in the software industry for years, and I didn't want to start contributing to something that had plagued my job in the past. Also, when you begin down this road, anti-virus software becomes a necessity—another purchase I really did not want to make.

For starters, as a former PC builder and tweaker, I'd learned quickly that nothing kills your performance quite as well as anti-virus software. Also, when running on a machine "infected" with anti-virus software, audio software is nonresponsive, buggy, and more. Don't get me started.

I conferred with a colleague or two about some alternatives to the missing software. I learned quickly that keeping the company of likeminded people (nerds like myself) was a great blessing, as I got my first introduction to open-source software and freeware. I also learned a valuable lesson that had somehow eluded me for years, perhaps out of pride: It's okay to ask questions.

One of the first software applications I learned about was Wavosaur. Even in its earliest incarnation, it was very powerful and was a viable replacement for Sound Forge. Also, it had batch processing, which was crucial, because I was going to be freelancing in videogames as well.

Did it work out? Wonderfully!

Next, I needed a replacement for some of my Waves software, the main plug-in being the L1. Thankfully, I learned of George Wong's W1 Limiter (mentioned in this book). This was a score, because I sorely needed it for mastering my remixes, and it's very handy for videogame batch processing as well.

Another problem solved, and zero dollars spent!

Next came the need to spruce up my personal FX section. In fact, it was going to need a complete overhaul. I'd need FX plug-ins that would give that instant cool-factor to my music, as well as FX that could also be used for videogames.

This is still an ongoing process, to be honest, because there are so many new FX coming up regularly, and your tastes change and music changes. You just collect like a painter with colors.

One effect I learned about early on and that changed my life (along with the lives of many others like me) is the Glitch plug-in, at the moment known as dB Glitch.

A friend of mine had completed a remix of my band for me. He completed it very quickly from the time I gave him the source material, and the results were astounding.

I inquired as to how he'd pulled off so many seemingly complex edits. This is when he shared a very big secret with me: It was just a plug-in known as Glitch.

At that particular moment of the plug-in's history, the creator had only *just* added a GUI (graphical user interface) to it. My friend had actually been using the command-line version. Being more of a graphics cat, I went with the GUI version.

I quickly learned that by simply throwing audio files into Glitch, letting it do its own thing in real time, and cutting out parts I liked, I could get amazing sound FX that I would have never thought of on my own. I began to slowly build up a collection of sounds that I could use over again and that would become staples in my sound library—available exclusively to me! Ha!

Also around this time, I began to miss a few synthesizers that I had hastily sold in a mad dash for money. Divorce and a major career change can bring on big decisions that you sometimes just have to live with. One such sell was my Roland Juno-106. It was such an authentic sound, and I'd relied on it heavily in my music work. Sad times, indeed...

Since I'd had so much luck with free plug-ins, I decided to see whether anyone had made a VST instrument that emulated a 106. After a few web searches, I came across the TAL U-NO-60 (also mentioned in this book). This plug was actually modeled after a Juno-60, but there are some strong similarities in the sound of the two synthesizers. I elected to give it a try. And you know what? It was so much fun!

The chorus was awesome, and just the behavior of the synth was so authentic. Even the GUI had the same look and feel as my recently departed synth. I shed a little tear.

Another synth that I was sorely missing was my Roland JP-8000. It was such a main tool when it came to doing lead synth lines and arpeggiations on my mixes. Granted, I had other soft synths that were sort of up to the challenge, but they weren't quite the same.

I decided to look around and hope that I had the same luck again.

Fortune smiled on me again; I came across the SuperWave P8. Seeing that it had earned a ton of positive reviews, I installed it and got going right away. Yep, there was the Supersaw that I'd been missing. My muse was back...well, at least the electronic one.

From here on out, I could tell you about discovery after discovery, all of which have some meaning to me. But the main point in writing this preface is to let you know what's out there if you just ask. To some degree, the freeware and open-source community has rekindled my faith in man. The fact that people would put so much time and love into something, only to turn around and share it with the rest of us who lack the coding skills to create such a thing, is, to me, quite beautiful.

I, in turn, have made every effort to give back in any small way that I can. Being a freelance author and musician isn't always the path to fame and fortune that some might think. But as money would come in, I'd drop a little back to the guys who helped me make things happen. I'm proud to say that I made a decent donation to these developers, and I hope that in some small way, I've helped them continue to develop software to help others like me.

# Acknowledgments

First and foremost, God—and then I'd like to thank every talented developer out there who ever decided to share the knowledge, code, and tools that they spent so much of their precious time on. This book would not be possible without your hard work, and it is meant to show off your talent, which is amazing.

Thanks to:

- Togu Audio Line. Guys, your stuff blows me away and really makes me want to play music.

- Johan Larsby at Shuriken.se. Your work is awesome, and your videos are hilarious. Love your stuff, man.

- Kieran Foster for Glitch over at illformed.org. As you did everyone else, you made a believer out of me.

- Peter Kirn at createdigitalmusic.com, for the wealth of knowledge he disseminates daily. You've been a true inspiration.

- Orren Merton, for continually giving me new opportunities!

- Cathleen Small, for keeping me on the path of the straight and narrow, keeping me on time, and keeping it fun!

- Michael Prager, for being a great friend, getting me into writing in the first place, and being my favorite person to see at NAMM.

- Josh Pyle, for his enthusiasm and longtime friendship.

- Joe Virus, for being a great guy, a great DJ, and a wonderful person with whom to have a long conversation about music.

- Rodney Orpheus, for introducing me to so much of all of this and for showing up at the oddest places. Parking lots, c'mon!

- Chris Petti, for many expensed dinners and introducing me to Lombardi's.

- Bob DeMaa, for the endless videogame conversations and *Halo* action.

- Josh Mobley, for the great interview. I hope we get to hang out at NAMM again soon!

- Ivan Cerillo, for having us down for a really fun show and a great interview.

- Don Hill, for a great interview and awesome music!

- Laura Escude, one of the most powerful musicians I know. A true force of nature that never stops. Great music and always moving. You're a badass.

- Steve Tushar, no interview, but I had a great time talking with you. Miss ya, man!

- My family: Bill, Suzanne, Alex, Allison, Jen, Tommy, Lexi, Haley, Will, Ruby, Judy, Andrew, Shelby, Warren, Amy, Caleb, and the twins! Tim and Cynthia.

- My friends, for just being friends: Christian Petke, Jay Tye, Ashley Horstman, Amrita Soni, Ramananda, Avoca Coffee, the Usual, Brick Purselly, Mr. and Mrs. Baron Purselly, Sherry Purselly, Butch Purselly, Buck Purselly. Ozzie Ozkay Villa, Mary Katherine Higgins, Dr. Edward Newsome, and Sera.

# About the Author

Starting off as a small boy on a farm in a galaxy far, far away, **G.W. Childs IV** dreamed of sound and music. As he grew, he learned synthesis, sound design, songwriting, and remixing. As a soldier in Psychological Operations, G.W. learned ways to creatively use sound. As a touring musician performing with the likes of Soil & Eclipse, Deathline Int'l, and Razed in Black, he learned to bring music to the masses.

Still listening to his inner child, G.W. decided to work in videogames as well, and he *really* stepped into a galaxy far, far away doing sound design on *Star Wars: Knights of the Old Republic II: The Sith Lords*, acting in *Star Wars: Battlefront*, and composing music for MTV's *I Woo You*.

But the call of synthesis never fully left his ears, so G.W. did a lot of sound design on the popular music applications Reason 3 and Reason 4 and the amazing Rapture plug-in from Cakewalk.

Excited to share knowledge from these wonderful adventures, he has written books such as *Creating Music and Sound for Games, Using Reason Onstage: Skill Pack*, and *Making Music with Mobile Devices*, in the hopes of inspiring other people in galaxies far, far away.

# Contents

# Chapter 4
# FX                                                                          55

# Chapter 5
# Drum Machines                                                               75

# Chapter 6
# Niche Plug-Ins                                                              95

## Chapter 7
## Where to Find More
**111**

## Appendix A
## More Must-Haves
**131**

## Appendix B
## Interviews with Laura Escudé and Don Hill
**165**

# Introduction

Let's face it—times are hard. Money doesn't roll in the way it used to for many of us, and the cost of living is not getting any lower. To make matters even more interesting, the computer is a necessary evil for almost all of us.

But despite challenging times, dreams still exist. People still dream of becoming the next president or the next great racecar driver or of achieving many other worthy and honorable careers and achievements.

Music is one such dream for many—especially with shows such as *American Idol* showcasing people like you and me taking a chance and suddenly becoming something that many dream of and few ever attain.

Music production is a monster that tends to hold many back, though—partly because of the uphill technical battle that goes along with it. But another factor is the daunting price of the music-production equipment.

However, most music-production devices now reside within the computer, instead of in heavy racks. This benefits those interested in music production in several ways:

- There are no longer physical manufacturing costs for these devices. The functionality is programmed instead, leading to a much quicker turnaround time and lower costs.
- Music production is now much more portable—and more affordable, due to the decreasing cost of laptops.
- There are no shipping costs. Most music software can be downloaded.

I'd like to give special attention to this final point about downloading. Almost all of the major developers offer downloadable versions of their music software directly from their websites. Simply pay for the product, and they send you a download link. It really doesn't get much better than that. If there's an update to the music software, you can download that, too.

The Internet has really changed the music-production industry, in much the same way that it changed how people listened to music years ago. Remember when the MP3 reared its trendy, compressed little head? Suddenly, people were downloading albums instead of running out to the stores to buy them. And because the music companies were not in any way ready for this, many fell.

But many artists benefited from this shift. Suddenly, people with a passion for creating music realized, "Hey, I can just put my music online, and now everyone can listen to it!" Granted, their strategies were much more complex than this, and with careful marketing strategies used by many aspiring young artists (and currently even mainstream artists), some power was taken away from the labels and given back to the artist. I'd like to tell you that at this moment—and for more years than you may know—even more power is available to the artist.

Unfortunately, music production is still a major challenge to overcome, though. You may have the fan base, but if your music sounds terrible or if you don't have the ability to produce music at all, that fan base will only scratch their heads as their interest wanes and they look elsewhere.

Even though music-production software has lowered the price of producing music, it is still expensive for many. But in the same way that artists found an audience on the Internet, intelligent and creative programmers found an audience as well.

Do you know that there are thousands of programmers out there trying to give you software that they have spent countless hours creating? I'm talking about software that can allow you to produce quality, professional music.

Why would they give it away, though? For the same reason that many artists give their music away! When you are a small-time artist, you can't just run out and ask people to buy your album. There are millions of other performers out there for people to choose from, so the chances of people buying your album when they've never heard of you are slim. Instead, you give away little bits at a time and build a name for yourself.

The same is true for software programmers. They are guys and gals like you and me who work from their homes on something that they think is a valid and helpful tool to assist musicians. And they would know, too, because music-software programmers tend to be musicians themselves!

The programmers want their tools and instruments to be used and loved in the same way that they use and love them. And hopefully, if they gain enough recognition in the field, they can move on and become professional developers.

In this book, I'll showcase many tools and instruments that are, in most cases, free. These aren't just Frankenstein pieces of software thrown together; they are lovingly created packages, instruments, and tools, made by people who love music just as much as you do and who weren't satisfied with what the pros were putting out. They decided to make their own software instead.

Before we proceed, I'd like to make one point clear: If you find yourself using a piece of software, an instrument, or a tool from this book a lot, kick a little money back to the developer if you can. These guys worked hard, and although most aren't expecting anything, as an artist you know how good it feels to get paid for your work!

And now, without further ado, let's get started building your free open-source music studio!

# 1 What You Need, What's Free, and What's Not

So, you've read this book's introduction, and you've decided, "Hey, I'd like to see what's out there." I'm so glad to hear it! Open-source music software offers some innovative and astoundingly cool applications, utilities, and plug-ins that really can add something to your sound—or just help you get a studio running when you're tight on cash.

I started investigating shareware and freeware plug-ins and applications years ago as a very, very poor family man who needed to support himself and his kid. Back then, it was difficult to get my wife to swallow the idea of paying $300 for software that would make my voice echo, given that we were having a tough time putting food on the table.

I'm not kidding when I tell you that one time I went on tour to Germany with only $50 to my name, while my wife was left with only $100. When I was getting my backing tracks together, I ended up using a shareware VST plug-in by db audioware as a compressor for my master tracks. It cost me $15, when all the other ones (cough, cough … *Native Instruments*) would have cost me a thousand.

Before I go farther, let me explain the difference between shareware and freeware.

## Shareware or Freeware?

*Shareware* is software that is relatively inexpensive and is far cheaper than software you'd buy from a major manufacturer. It usually costs $100 to $200 less than software from a major manufacturer.

1

*Freeware* is software that does not cost anything at all. Zip! Zilch! And, rest assured, I will do my best to point you toward freeware in almost all instances. However, there will be times when I'll point you to inexpensive software as well, if it's an app or plug-in that I think will assist you.

Which brings us to apps and plug-ins...

## What Are Apps? What Are Plugs-Ins?

*Apps*, or *applications*, are standalone programs that you can install on your computer that do not require any secondary software. They run on their own, and that's that.

*Plug-ins* are supplemental applications that run inside certain types of applications. Think of an application like a studio, and the plug-in as either an instrument (such as a synthesizer or a bass guitar) or an FX processor (such as an echo for your voice). Essentially, the plug-ins only work inside of an application—*host application* is a term you'll hear me use throughout the book.

There are also different types of plug-ins. One good thing about plug-ins is that they are very small and quick to download. Finding and downloading a plug-in is like finding an amplifier online for free and then having someone deliver it to you instantly!

Plug-in types include:

- VST (*Virtual Studio Technology*) for Mac and PC
- AU (*Audio Units*) for Mac only
- DX (*DirectX*) for PC only

Keep in mind that although you may find yourself with a new habit of looking around for free software, you'll spend a lot more time looking around for plug-ins. There are literally thousands upon thousands out there for free, as you will find out in many of the chapters that are waiting for you farther along in the book.

## What Will I Need to Get Started?

Although I can direct you to tons of cheap and free software online, there is nothing I can do for you in terms of hardware. Unfortunately, the Internet does not currently support teleportation (the ability to instantly transport a piece of matter from one location to another, for you guys and gals who never watched *Star Trek*). So instead, I would like to recommend some hardware that you will want to look into.

### Computer

First and foremost, you will need a regular computer. And yes, you definitely want to go with a newer computer that can stand up to the rigors of computer audio.

It is also important to note that the type of computer you choose (Mac or PC) will have lasting implications on what software you use (to a degree). Let's take a quick look at each platform.

#### *Mac*

Apple may come off as the most expensive choice initially. However, Apple handles some costs right off the bat that you might want to be aware of.

The setup is painless. There's no need to worry about driver installation, strange tweaks to the system software, and so on. Apple takes the work out of using a computer, and if you're new to computer audio, there is a lot to be said for this. After all, you're buying the computer to do music, to use it as a tool for creativity—not to take a long journey into computer programming, hacking, and so on. For the most part, when you crack open a new Apple computer, everything is already set up and ready to go.

Also, the Apple brand has been a proven success for audio production over a period of many, many years. Most professional musicians, producers, and engineers have been very open about their love of the

Apple platform, almost to the point of zealotry. With good reason, too: stable computer = unbridled creativity = music at its best = good shot at success.

Seriously, think about it. These days, a computer crashing can kill an album entirely, setting you back for weeks or even months. What you record is precious, and trying to re-create it after the moment is lost is not always a possibility. I've had this happen to me more than once, and I do need to point out that I was on a PC each time it occurred. I've had a Mac go down on me, too; however, I'll admit that I'd been putting the machine through hell for years. The PC was brand-new!

Another point I'd like to make is that the Mac can run Windows, Linux, and every other OS under the sun. People have created "Hackintosh" PCs that run the Mac OS, but if you read the guides for doing this, it's not for the faint of heart. Mac OS X Leopard and Snow Leopard both have Boot Camp, a small application and driver set that helps you set up Windows on a separate partition. When you launch the Windows partition, it's as if you are using a PC. And, in fact, you are—until you reboot and go back into OS X.

Finally, in terms of cost, these days there are plenty of different types of Apples with different price tags to go along with them. For example, at the time of this writing, a Mac mini lists for $699. It is quite powerful for a computer that is smaller than a football. Something to think about...

Also, because most of the viruses that are being created by the lonely, bitter hackers out there are for the Windows platform, Mac users have enjoyed far more of their system resources. Virus applications use system resources in the background, which interferes with audio applications, and they usually require a monthly, quarterly, or yearly service fee.

I recommend going with new when it comes to computers, because the software is always being upgraded—even freeware. Each upgrade usually means harsher system requirements. Having a new machine means that you won't be left out in the cold.

If you do buy a used Mac, make sure that it has at least these features:

- **An Intel Core 2 Duo processor.** You may see great deals on used G5-based Apple computers, but I advise against purchasing one. The G5 had a lot of heat problems, and they do not compare to the processing power of the Intel-based Macs.

- **CD/DVD player and burner.** Many music apps come on DVDs these days, and you want to be able to burn your songs onto a CD, right?

- **At least 2 GB of system memory with the option to upgrade to 4 GB.** Audio apps, plug-ins, and so on use a lot of system memory, so the more you have, the smoother your productions will be.

---

**Note:** Did you know that Apple computers already come with a pretty formidable audio application, right out of the box? GarageBand, covered briefly in Chapter 2, "DAW," is an extremely powerful audio application with virtual instruments, the ability to record multiple tracks, and even piano and guitar lessons hosted by celebrities!

---

## PC

If you wish to go with a PC (and there is nothing wrong with that), I need to point out a few realities.

- If you are new to computers, have a friend who is very experienced with computer installation give you a hand with getting your machine up and running. Have him actually look at the manuals, too, because audio applications can have some quirky installations at times.

- Be very aware of the ports on the desktop or laptop you purchase. You'll need at least two USB 2.0 ports, and a FireWire port is advisable as well. Many audio interfaces use FireWire.

- Dell, HP, and Sony are all reputable names on the PC market. You might ask around on the forums for various audio applications you are interested in and see whether people can advise you on a model, a company, or a home-built machine with internal parts that they recommend. It is not uncommon for a particular chipset on a PC to cause problems with certain audio interfaces, applications, and so on.

■ Although virus protection software is advisable while you are working on the Windows platform, keep in mind that virus software does not play well with most audio applications. In almost all cases, developers of shareware, freeware, and commercial applications advise you to disable virus software while using audio software.

Aside from these warnings, PCs actually have something very big going for them: There is a ton of shareware and freeware software available for PCs. However, as mentioned earlier, Macs can run this software too, if you Boot Camp your Mac. On the flip side, PCs cannot easily run Apple software. Having a computer that can do both gives you that much more software!

## Audio Interface

Another device I highly advise purchasing is an audio interface. This device simply sends audio to your speakers and gives you additional connections for microphones, guitars, and so on.

You might be wondering why you can't use the connections built into your computer. Well, there are several reasons for that:

■ You most likely have only the small, 1/8-inch connections on your computer. If you try to hook a guitar to that, well...it will be a bit big when you try to use a 1/4-inch connector there (see Figure 1.1).

■ The audio driver supplied by your computer's manufacturer may not be up for audio recording. On a PC, the ASIO driver format is the standard for all audio recording software; this also comes into play if you're using virtual instruments. If you don't have hardware that has an ASIO driver on a PC, you're stuck using WDM,

**Figure 1.1** If you try to plug a guitar cord (1/4-inch) into this input, it won't fit.

DirectX, or other drivers that can be equally slow and useless for computer audio. This will result in you pressing a key on your keyboard and then waiting a second to hear the sound. Also, you'll get severely lagging audio performance behind the music. It can get ugly.

■ The built-in input not only is small, but it also is only one input. What if you want to record two inputs or more at the same time?

The bottom line is that an audio interface is a worthwhile investment if you want to start off right and you don't want to risk pulling out your hair by trying to make a Windows driver work.

If you are using a Mac, you can squeak by for a while with the Core Audio driver for your internal sound device; it has great latency for a built-in sound adapter. However, as mentioned earlier, this will get tricky when you want to directly connect your new mic, guitar, and so on.

Back to keeping it cheap … Audio interfaces have a broad price range. For example, the Behringer UCA222 is a small, USB audio adapter that will do the basic job wonderfully, and it only costs around $50 (see Figure 1.2).

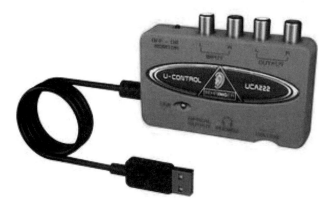

**Figure 1.2** The Behringer UCA22 is a very small, lightweight audio interface that costs barely a quarter of your car payment.

If you have a little more money to play with and you want something on the higher end of the spectrum, the Apogee Duet ($495) is a wonderfully simple audio interface that sports some of the best audio converters in the industry (see Figure 1.3). Note that Apogee has PC drivers, but it only truly supports Apple computers these days.

These are only a few of the hundreds of audio interfaces that exist. Many local music stores have specialists who would be happy to help you choose the appropriate audio interface for you. Or, even better, consult user forums for software apps that interest you and ask what other people are using before you take the plunge.

## MIDI Controller
The final device that I recommend you pick up before embarking on the journey of computer-based music—with open-source software, freeware, and so on—would be a MIDI controller.

**Figure 1.3** The Apogee Duet is an amazing, pint-sized audio interface that uses the world-famous Apogee audio converters.

A MIDI controller is simply a musical keyboard that plugs into your computer via USB. What differentiates a USB MIDI controller from your old Casio is that it doesn't require any special port, it does not make any sounds of its own, and it usually will have additional knobs and buttons that give you the ability to control other parameters and functions within the software you use.

MIDI controllers range in price, like audio interfaces do, but they are actually the cheaper purchase of the two.

Even if you are a guitarist or a drummer, you will still want to invest in one of these devices for these reasons:

- I sincerely doubt that all of your songs will consist only of drums and guitar. You may say that is true now, but I bet it changes down the line.

- You will most likely want to add other instruments, such as piano, strings, and so on.

- A MIDI controller can also assist you in editing your drums, automation, and so on in ways you might not have considered.

For example, a kick drum might be assigned to C1 on the keyboard, and then you can add in a few extra fills just by pressing the keyboard a couple of times.

M-Audio makes a huge line of MIDI controllers that range in price. Controllers such as the Axiom 25 are small, light, and relatively inexpensive (less than $200, as of this writing). See Figure 1.4.

**Figure 1.4** The Axiom 25 is not only a great keyboard controller, but it also features drum pads!

Also, the Axiom 25 sports some really sturdy pads on the upper-left corner of the unit that you can use for tapping in drums and so on.

This is a controller I've had a lot of luck with, but if you look through the piles of keyboard controllers available at Guitar Center, Sam Ash, and other fine music establishments, I guarantee you will find one that will do the job at the right price.

How about the nanoKEY from Korg (see Figure 1.5)? It's maybe the length of a forearm and almost as thin as your wallet in the current recession. It weighs three pounds, at most. This little gem lists for $50,

**Figure 1.5** The nanoKey is a small, fully functional MIDI controller with a price tag that will make you jump for joy!

as of this writing. However, I have news for you. I got mine for $30 online. How's that for a steal?

I also encourage you to explore the rest of the Korg Nano line. There are portable devices to fit most of your recording needs. Check out www.korgusa.com.

## Do I Need to Worry about Viruses?

Now that I've given you a walkthrough of hardware devices you'll need for recording music on a home computer, let's talk about something that, as I explained earlier, really only applies to non-Apple computers—viruses. However, because Apple computers are becoming more common as Apple grows in power and in the stock market, you should still be smart in what you download.

Viruses generally are picked up when you are:

- Cruising for illegally uploaded software or pirated software.

- Visiting websites that host material that is already suspect due to its content—for example, many websites that host "Get Rich Quick" schemes that you come across by pressing random links, websites that host "How I Lost 75 Pounds in 10 Days" types of content, or websites that, in fact, host "Free Virus Protection."

- Clicking random links without taking the time to think about whether you actually know the company website that it's pointing to.

- Visiting websites that host pornography of any sort.

If you partake in any of these activities, you have two options. First, get yourself virus protection. Norton or any one of a number of others will do the trick, but remember to turn off the virus protection when you're making music. Second, use another machine for this kind of practice. Many people have one machine for music and one machine for office work, email, and cruising the Internet.

Bottom line: Be smart in what websites you visit. If it sounds too good to be true, it may be too good to be true, and it may give you a big, fat headache of a night while you reformat your hard drive, reinstall all your software, and so on.

## Will Open-Source Apps Break My Computer?

Wondering whether free or cheap software will harm your computer is a very valid concern. The simple fact is that *any* software can introduce instability to your computer. But if you read the manuals and "read me" documents and follow them the way you are supposed to, most likely you will never experience any problems. I've screened the software that is being presented in this book, and I haven't had any problems whatsoever. However, I've been doing this for a long time. Bottom line: If you aren't sure, have a friend help you who is!

## How Do Open-Source Apps and Plug-Ins Compete?

Now that you have a better idea of what you'll need to get going, let's talk about the fun part: music software!

The first question I would ask is basically the same as the title of this section: How do open-source, shareware, and freeware apps compete with commercial software?

As most of our society is assimilated into the Internet, along with our commerce, mating rituals, social interactions, and sometimes spiritual beliefs, you will begin to notice that even commercially made software is starting to become available for purchase and immediate download. That should say something right there: The commercial software makers are starting to do away with boxes! So, if commercial manufacturers are doing away with boxes and making their software available for immediate download upon purchase, why is this any different from supporting the little guy?

Keep in mind that many amazingly talented people are out of work right now. This gives some of them time to make money on the side using hobbies, prior training, and more. These individuals are unencumbered by meetings, coworkers, and budgets. They can put a greater amount of time into developing software than a company might want to pay for. Also, by not having coworkers to collaborate with, people can follow their instincts on what's cool, rather than having to develop what a group of people thinks might be cool.

The end result is fresh software that may sport features that a company never considered. And you are getting to it first!

I have more freeware plug-ins than I can count on all my fingers. I use more full apps that I downloaded for free (legally) than I can list completely in this book. (Do you really want to hear about what I use to balance my checkbook?) Many of these plug-ins or apps are pieces of software I would definitely have on a remote island, along with my imaginary friend.

So learn this lesson: Just because it's cheap or free, that doesn't mean it's crap!

The developers who put their time into shareware, freeware, and open-source software are just as passionate as the major corporate developers. They have new ideas, they care about their work, and they want their product to be used!

So, why is it free or cheap? Hey, you have to start somewhere right? With e-commerce, a proven marketing trick is to give away something for free so that you create a familiarity with your work. When a free customer is familiar with you, they are more likely to buy something later. Use this strategy to your advantage. They are nice little carrots dangling out there. Grab a bite and try them out!

## Money

Although this book endeavors to keep things cheap (but good at the same time), I will show you some software that does cost money. However, you can rest assured that either there is a demo version that has great value or the price tag is quite low.

Also, remember, the developers highlighted in this book are passionate, artistic, funny, kind, and…human. We're all trying to make a buck right now. If you download a synth that costs you nothing and you use it all the time, go back to the developer's website and locate a "PayPal Donate" link. Kick a couple of bucks to these guys and gals! Who knows? The happy smiles that come across their faces could lead to another piece of software that you may fall in love with later. It may even supply the final polish that helps you make that top-ten single that earns you millions. It could happen!

## Conclusion

Now you know what you need. You also know that your computer will not blow up if you install something that Apple or Microsoft didn't make. You've also learned that you should be smart about where you go on the Internet, and you know what hardware you'll need to continue. The main piece of hardware is the computer, and beyond that you can always buy as you need.

In the next chapter, we'll discuss the big apps: digital audio workstations (DAWs). These are the first apps you'll need to get started!

**Interview with Bob DeMaa**

**Could you give us a quick introduction with some of the albums, software packages, and singles you've been a part of?**

My name is Bob DeMaa, and I've been working with software and computers since 1983. I started engineering professionally in 1993, and since then I have mastered thousands of tracks and engineered many albums. Probably one of my favorite albums to work on was the soundtrack for *Monster's Ball*, composed by Asche & Spencer Music, where I mixed and mastered the soundtrack. Much of the work for albums I do is mastering work, mainly with independent artists. Some of the recent albums I've worked on were for Rusty Truck (surround), Farflung, Two Guns, the Branches, and New Eyes. I've mixed recent albums for Rie Sinclair (*A Moment You Never Dreamed*) and Quitters Go to Meetings (*Talkback-drums*). Most of the work I do, though, is for composers for whom I mix and master. I've mastered or mixed for several libraries' worth of music for Asche & Spencer, Music Box, and Endless Noise.

Software-wise I have beta-tested for SSL Duende, Euphonix Artist Series, and Ohm Force Ohm Studio, and I've made several tutorial videos showing functionality of Logic and Pro Tools. I also wrote a clinic for Ozone, on which I received a lot of great feedback.

**How much experience have you had with free or open-source music plug-ins?**

I try every plug-in eventually. Demo periods are often short, so I try to time it where I can really experience the sound of the plug-in, and I'm often surprised by how much I do or don't like particular plug-ins, regardless of the marketing that may or may not coincide with the plug-in.

**Is there a particular audio plug-in of which you are extremely fond? Feel free to list multiple ones.**

Plug-ins I rely on and love for mixing, in no particular order, include:

- isotope: Ozone and Alloy
- Stillwell Audio: Bombardier, Rocket, and 1973
- UAD: LA-2A, 1176, Fatso Sr., dbx 160
- GRM Tools
- SoundToys: All of them!
- Brainworx: Digital V2
- Audio Ease: Altiverb
- Audio Pluggers: K-Meter
- Blue Cat Audio: Widening Gain
- SSL: Bus Compressor, Drumstrip
- PSP: VintageWarmer 2
- Nomad Factory: Brickwall BW25-3, Analog Chorus CH25-3
- IK Multimedia: ARC
- Crysonic: Spectralive
- Ceremony: Melodyne
- Native Instruments: KORE and all its FX packages

Synth plug-ins I love include:

- U-he: Zebra2
- Waldorf: Largo
- Spectrasonics: Omnisphere
- Native Instruments: KORE, KONTAKT, BATTERY

- Sonic Charge: MicroTonic

- Cakewalk: Dimension Pro

- Arturia Jupiter-8V2

- Logic: Sculpture, ES1, ES2, Ultrabeat

**Could you share a quick story about where this plug-in has really shined during your music creation/production work?**

It's hard to pinpoint any one plug-in as carrying more load overall, but I'd have to say the most mileage goes to Ozone 4. It's not something I mix on, but when used very subtly, it always brings the mix to that final-level polish and sweetness that just hits the spot. I use it all the time, and it's a very effective, very fast way to dial in that last stage of the mix just right.

I'm also really impressed by the Stillwell Audio plug-ins. They sound great, work great, and are very affordable with no demo limit. Guys as cool and talented as these deserve the $30 to $50 they ask for donation.

**Is there a particular free/open-source virtual instrument of which you've become fond? Feel free to list multiple ones.**

Green Oak Crystal is an awesome free synth. With a couple of quick adjustments, you can get some great sounds out of it. I've been using this one for years.

**Could you share a quick story about where this instrument has really shined during your music creation/ production work?**

I've gotten some great, trippy sounds out of it, and it always layers nicely with other synths. I rarely use just a single synth for a part. Maybe that goes back to the early '90s, when synths were thinner-sounding and not as spatially complex as they can be now, but I still layer two to four sounds for a part and then fluctuate them slightly during a mix to provide the part with some variation. Crystal works quite well for this.

**Have you had any difficulties installing or working with any of the free/open-source plug-ins that you've checked out?**

No, but I've been installing software for 25 years. These days, most of them have simple installers that do the work for you, or simply dragging and dropping a component or VST to the correct folder is all it takes.

**Do you have any advice for beginner musicians/ producers working with free/open-source audio plug-ins?**

Respect the hand that feeds. Coding and getting everything right is hard work. You may not like a plug-in or you may be frustrated by something it does or doesn't do, but that's no reason to be hating on it. Have fun experimenting, close your eyes, and listen to it. A/B the track or mix with it on and off. Is it really doing what you think it is? It is not easy to separate the marketing and comments about a plug-in's ability from its actual sound and use in your music. Test it thoroughly, and if it isn't for you, then get something else to experiment with, because honestly, that's the fun part!

Excellent resources for new and old plug-ins are macmusic. org and kvraudio.com. I suggest subscribing to their RSS feeds to stay in touch with new software as it's released, as well as using them for plug-in reference. Both are fantastic sources of info.

# 2 DAWs

In building a music system, one piece of software is central before it can all start to happen: the DAW (*digital audio workstation*) or host software. The DAW is the place where you sculpt and form your ideas. Artists have Photoshop, a virtual canvas where they can build anything their mind can process. Musicians have DAWs that allow them to craft, play, and arrange until they have a song.

DAWs allow more than one kind of recording. Yes, they record audio like a tape recorder, so you can hear yourself singing. And yes, they also record multiple tracks of audio, so you can hear yourself singing along with backup tracks of you supporting your original vocal line. But there is one more oh-so-important thing that they record: MIDI.

MIDI stands for *Musical Instrument Digital Interface*. Whereas recording audio actually takes in your voice through a microphone and captures the audio digitally on your hard drive, MIDI records something else. For example, with a MIDI keyboard, you start recording what you are playing. It is a happy melody with a lot of feeling and emotion. When you press a key and look at the computer, you notice that little ticks are displayed with every key press. When you are finished playing your happy melody, you see a collage of tick marks in a string on the computer screen.

The ticks (as I like to call them) are what are recorded in MIDI. To explain it even better, when you record MIDI, you aren't actually recording sound; the computer is recording the key you pressed, how hard you pressed the key, and the timing at which you pressed the key.

If this seems confusing, there are countless books on MIDI available. But in my opinion, the best way to learn about it is to use it. So, let's get to work on finding a suitable DAW for you so that you can get started!

# Shareware and Freeware DAWs

It's amazing to me that freeware/shareware DAWs even exist. I can't even tell you the amount of money I've spent in the past on just such software. It isn't pretty!

In this chapter, I'll showcase some really amazing pieces of software that do all (or most of) the same things the commercial DAWs (such as Pro Tools, Cubase, and so on) do. But because all of these are made by individuals like you and me, you may find some features, once you start trying these out, that the professional packages don't have.

## Ardour (Mac/Linux)

I can tell you what the most money I ever spent on a DAW was: $500, give or take. Yes, I got my money's worth out of it, and yes, I enjoyed it. It was full featured, and it was impressive, but it was 1998—everything was pretty impressive back then.

When I bought Ardour (yes, I said "bought," but hear me out), I was impressed by its interface, its ease of use, and its feature set. By the way, this feature set keeps up with everything out there and is light years ahead of what I paid $500 for back in 1998.

So how much did I spend on Ardour? Two hundred dollars? Three hundred? Nope—ten dollars. The developers of Ardour give you the option to choose what you want to pay. You can also choose not to pay, but if you do this, you'll get a lighter version of Ardour that lacks many essential features.

So, what do you get with Ardour?

- **Unlimited audio tracks.** That might sound trivial at first, but a lot of the freebie applications will limit you.

**Figure 2.1** Ardour is a full-fledged studio for which you can pay literally any price you want!

- **Unlimited undos.** Suppose you delete a vocal recording, only to realize a few minutes later that you deleted the wrong one. However, you've done several edits since then. What do you do? Press the Undo button until the vocal recording reappears. Usually it's either Command+Z on a Mac or Ctrl+Z on a PC.

- **VST plug-in functionality.** If you're running the Linux version of Ardour, you have the ability to employ Windows VST plug-ins, which is huge.

- **Video-synced playback.** You can actually score movies in this free software. There are other applications I won't even mention that make you pay additional money for this feature.

- **Audio Unit support.** For Mac users, there is Audio Unit support. There are quite a few free AU plug-ins out there, which I'll cover in later chapters in this book.

- **Free plug-ins.** More than 200 free plug-ins come with Ardour right off the bat.

Because Ardour is still in development, it currently has very limited MIDI implementation. At present, you can do MIDI clicks and machine control, but you cannot record MIDI instruments, or software instruments. However, this is planned for Ardour 3, which is still in development. See www.ardour.org.

## MU.LAB (PC and Mac)

I love applications, such as Reason, that give you extensive capability to route your instruments, to create new instruments, and so on. So, I was very pleased when I came across MU.LAB (www.mutools.com). Not only does MU.LAB have a beautiful and simple interface, it also cleverly conceals some very advanced features (see Figure 2.2).

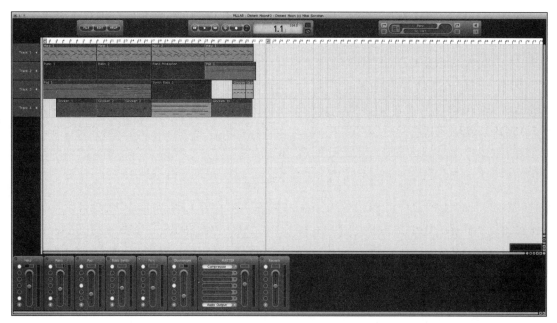

**Figure 2.2** MU.LAB has several variations that you can purchase. One of them is actually free and does quite a bit.

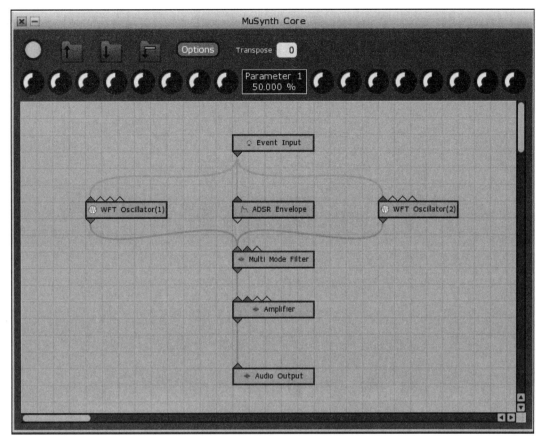

**Figure 2.3**  Create your own instruments in MU.LAB.

The most appealing of these features (to me, at least) is the ability to create your own synthesizers with MU.LAB's built-in synthesizer engine. Similarly to Logic Pro's environment, you can drag out different modules, such as oscillators, ADSR envelopes, filters, and so on (see Figure 2.3). Then you can route and configure these modules in interesting and fun ways until you have the synthesizer you desire.

But don't let me give you the idea that MU.LAB is all about synthesizers. You do get audio tracks. The free version limits you to four tracks, but the savvy musician can go a long way on just four tracks. Essentially, that's enough for vocals and three synth parts.

If you are willing to spend a bit more, you can unlock the full version of MU.LAB. This version costs $75 (as of this writing)—a very small price to pay for unlimited tracks and a synth engine like the one MU.LAB offers. Or, for $25, you can update to MU.LAB XT, which will upgrade you to eight tracks.

One thing I was very impressed with is the quality of the tutorial videos that MU.LAB developers (MUTOOLS) have made available on their website. They are quality, and you can tell that the developers really want people to understand their products. If you are new to computer music, this would be a great starting point for you.

## Audacity (PC, Mac, and Linux)

Although Audacity (audacity.sourceforge.net) isn't a full-fledged DAW, don't overlook its relevance. Audacity is one of the most famous open-source audio applications out there (see Figure 2.4). It's easy to use, allows quick and easy nondestructive and destructive edits, and is absolutely free.

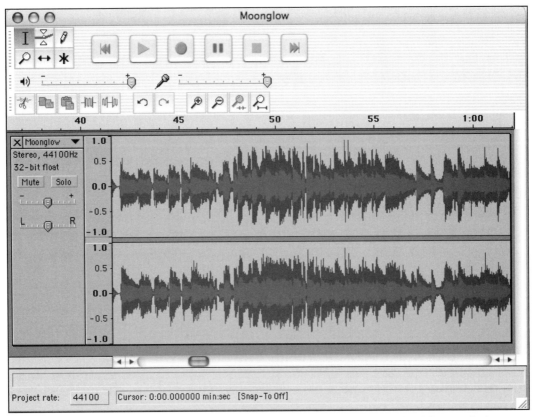

**Figure 2.4** Audacity is one of the most feature-filled and oldest of the open-source audio applications.

Audacity gives you unlimited audio tracks and the ability to record up to 16 audio tracks at once. It also gives you cool abilities, such as WAV/AIF to MP3 conversion, which you'll want if you plan to share your songs with your friends.

But here's where it gets even better: You can record from 16-bit (CD quality) on up to 32-bit. And, you can record in sample rates up to 96 kHz.

With Audacity, you have the ability to use VST plug-ins for either Mac or PC with the VST Enabler. But what's also impressive is that Audacity comes with quite a few plug-ins of its own. This includes classic effects, such as echo, phaser, wah wah, and reverse. But there are also necessary effects, such as compressor, amplify, and equalization.

Because Audacity is one of the most feature-filled free DAWs and does not require any fee whatsoever, it should be your starting point in determining what is right for you. Audacity doesn't do any MIDI, but if you are doing simple rock or acoustic works, it's perfect for you.

## Cost-Effective Commercial Options

If these free platforms don't do it for you, I'd like to draw your attention to some DAW packages that cost a small amount of money. However, before you purchase, there is usually a demo version of these applications so you can evaluate them before you spend any money. And believe me, if there's one piece of software you want to be absolutely sure you are comfortable with and enjoy, it's the DAW. Everything else is negotiable.

### REAPER (PC and Mac)

REAPER (www.reaper.fm) is a steal, especially for the starting musician. For one thing, Cockos (the company that develops REAPER) offers a fair-pricing deal up front. If you are an individual using REAPER for personal use, it costs $40. If you are a business and your yearly gross revenue does not exceed $20,000, your price is $40. Not bad, eh?

**Figure 2.5** REAPER is a very cool DAW package with a price that will make you sing.

But beyond price, REAPER has gained steady ground as the DAW software package of choice for many (see Figure 2.5).

I greatly admire Cockos's mindset and goal. When you buy REAPER, you purchase it online; it's a tiny download. This is just a byproduct of their goal of keeping the overhead low and keeping the price reasonable—and with no engineering compromises.

But what about REAPER itself? It's fully 64-bit compatible, with a wonderfully fluid drag-and-drop feature. Simply drag in an audio or MIDI file, and REAPER will prepare a track—there's no going through menus and so on. REAPER is also ReWire-compliant, so you can use other ReWire-based applications along with it. And you can do real-time network FX processing. In this instance, you're essentially using multiple computers on your network to help you process those massive effects you've instantiated.

Although all of this is cool, let me take a step back and talk about the interface. REAPER is very similar to Pro Tools in its feel and layout. But in my opinion, it also has things laid out in a clearer, more intuitive fashion. And it is highly customizable. There are different skins available that provide different color palettes and more.

Did I mention it has global time compression? At any point, you can slow down the rate of the song, and the audio just slows down along with it. This is very similar to Ableton Live.

Because REAPER has a free 30-day trial version available, it would behoove you to check it out. This version is uncrippled and gives you everything—you can save, load, and so on.

Seriously, check out this DAW even before the free ones, even before some of the others, and especially if you have some Pro Tools background. You will not regret it!

---

**Note:** If you decide you like REAPER and you want to learn more about how to use all of its features to their maximum potential, check out *REAPER Power!: The Comprehensive Guide* (Course Technology PTR, 2009).

---

## GarageBand (Mac)

When you purchase an Apple computer, you get one thing no other computer offers right out of the box: the ability to make music.

GarageBand comes with every current Apple computer, and it is far more powerful than you might think (see Figure 2.6). Developed by the same team that developed Logic Pro, GarageBand has many of the same features, just made more intuitive for beginners.

Time-stretching and pitch-shifting are done in key and easily in the background, so that you can change the included guitar loops, bass loops, and more to the key in which you're currently working. And you can easily adjust the speed of loops by simply adjusting the tempo of your project. GarageBand adapts to your needs as you work.

But beyond simple features, GarageBand teaches you as well. Garage-Band includes tons of tutorials that teach you how to play songs, read

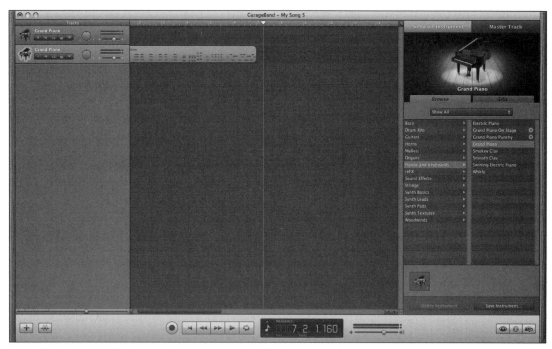

**Figure 2.6** If you own a Mac and are new to music software, do not underestimate GarageBand.

music, and more. And these tutorials are given not only by seasoned trainers, but also by major artists, such as Sting.

GarageBand also has some more advanced features as well, such as automation. Using automation, you can easily program a track to fade out at specified points, lower vocals in a certain part of your song, and more. Also, there are several software instruments, drum kits, and more available.

Right out of the box, your Apple computer will allow you to make a fine-sounding song that might surprise many professionals with its quality.

Another feature worth mentioning is that GarageBand works seamlessly with other Apple applications, such as iTunes, iMovie, iDVD, and more. You essentially get a one-stop shop for multimedia as soon as you buy a Mac.

**Note:** If you decide you like GarageBand and you want to learn more about how to use all of its features to their maximum potential, check out *GarageBand Power!: The Comprehensive Recording and Podcasting Guide* (Course Technology PTR, 2011).

## Ableton Live Intro (PC and Mac)

If you think you may be using loops or DJing, or you just like some extra tweakability, you may want to consider Ableton Live Intro (www.ableton.com). See Figure 2.7.

**Figure 2.7** Ableton is a major player that offers some affordable and helpful packages.

Ableton Live Intro is the most expensive of any packages listed in this chapter (it's $99 for online purchase), but hear me out. Your $99 gets you the majority of Ableton Live features, period.

Ableton Live Intro is limited on audio tracks, but only up to 64. It's a lot of work to get up to 64 tracks, believe me. But beyond that, you have a very powerful program that is as flexible as the day is long.

Ableton Live is amazing in the sense that you can import any audio into it, and it will automatically "warp" the audio so that it matches your song's tempo. This is a prized feature for many DJs out there, and that's what has made Ableton into one of the strongest packages available for DJs. And with "the Bridge" out now, you can also use Ableton with Serato, a very well-known DJ interface and application.

Before you download anything, here's something to keep in mind: Ableton offers a 30-day free trial of their software (any package) from their website. With each package (including Intro), there are tutorials galore to instruct you in using Ableton Live. This is perfect if you're new to computer audio, and let me tell you, the tutorials are done quite well.

The trials give you full access to all of the instruments, effects, and so on that come with Ableton, and you can learn to your heart's content. Once you're a champ, determine which package you think will work best for you.

---

**Note:** If you decide you like Ableton Live and you want to learn more about how to use all of its features to their maximum potential, check out *Your Ableton Live Studio* (Course Technology PTR, 2010).

---

## Conclusion

Because DAWs are large and complex software applications to put together, there aren't actually a ton of free ones out there. However, the ones that are available are formidable, and you should take them seriously as you move forward as a new musician/producer—or as a seasoned veteran who's tired of paying ridiculously high upgrade fees.

In closing, before you make any purchase, should you choose to go that route, always test the software extensively. Spend some time with it and see what you think.

As you are researching applications, remember that there are almost always forums on developer websites that are filled with users who can give you tips and more information.

### Interview with Chris Petti

**Could you give us a quick introduction with some of the albums, software packages, and singles you've been a part of?**

My name is Chris Petti. I am a graduate of Berklee College of Music's Music Synthesis bachelor's degree program. I have been involved with several of the major music manufacturers (Korg, Line 6, Propellerhead) over the past 10 years, working as a demonstrator, and I've had some sound/preset programming projects along the way. Currently, I teach electronic music production at Dubspot in NYC. Over the years, I have been involved in remixes, commercial, radio, and post-production projects. I also write original tunes but have not had any major album releases.

**How much experience have you had with free or open-source music plug-ins?**

I've had quite a bit of experience with free music-making plug-ins and freeware apps, some of which have really surprised me with their quality, stability, and functionality.

**Is there a particular audio plug-in of which you are extremely fond? Feel free to list multiple ones.**

I am extremely fond of the TAL plug-ins by Togu Audio Line—specifically the BassLine, U-No-62, NoiseMaker, and Elek7ro. The BassLine is an emulation of the SH-101; U-No-62 is the Juno-60; Elek7ro is a two-osc analog-style synth with FM and sync; and NoiseMaker is a two-osc analog-style synth with FM, sync, ring mod, chorus, and a very cool low-fi'er that is great for getting dirty bass sounds. Many of the effects processors are great, too—especially the Chorus 60, which is the chorus off of the Juno 60. I use the TAL plug-ins in classroom scenarios, too.

I have always been a huge fan of the Roland synths from the 1980s, and you can probably imagine how heart-broken I have been that Roland has not yet released plug-in versions of their legacy of synths. I was thrilled when I found the TAL plugs. My first synth was a Juno-106. This was what I learned synthesis on. I still have the original, but it doesn't get as much playtime as it once did, thanks to the modern conveniences of software instruments. The TAL version is pretty accurate in many respects to the Juno series.

Installing the TAL plug-ins can be a little weird if you are unfamiliar with where AU/VST plug-ins get placed in OS X. There is no installer for the package. The components and VST files must be placed in the Audio Plug-Ins folder.

My other favorite freeware music tool is Soundhack, written by Tom Erbe. I was first exposed to this at Berklee by Dr. Richard Boulanger, my DSP professor. Soundhack allows you to perform a number of complex functions on digital audio, but it doesn't work as a plug-in. I have been using it ever since Berklee to mangle and twist new sounds out of digital audio. I then fly the results into my sampler and turn them into patches.

I use Soundhack on nearly every tune I work on to create very original-sounding textures and music beds. I had been working on a Dubstep tune several months ago with a friend with whom I collaborate. The track called for a very organic, almost alive-sounding analog synth/string pad. I could hear it in my head, but I wasn't able to create the sound easily with some of my other instruments. Really, what I was hearing was the very lush and identifiable chorus produced by the Juno on a simple analog synth/string pad. I was able to easily dial up the sound very quickly on the U-No-62.

**Have you had any difficulties installing or working with any of the free/open-source plug-ins that you've checked out?**

I have not had any issues that I can think of with stability or inconsistencies.

**Do you have any advice for beginner musicians/ producers working with free/open-source audio plug-ins?**

For beginners, I suggest exploring the free plug-ins and music freeware that exist. Much of it doesn't always stand up to commercial plug-ins, but there are some gems out there. Remember, not too long ago, people were making great music with much less gear. They had to get very creative with the limited set of what existed.

# 3 Synthesizers

One of my favorite types of free plug-in—in fact, the type that I find myself looking for most often—is the software synthesizer. Even if you aren't a keyboardist, you have to admit that there's a lot to love there. A new software synthesizer means:

- A range of new sounds to include bells, pads, pianos, and more

- Cool rhythm generators, such as arpeggiators, LFOs, gates, and so on

- Potentially new types of synthesis that can be added to your compositions, giving your sounds that extra something you might have been missing

But before we jump into the whole mess of software synthesizers, I'd like to give you a little incentive to appreciate the knowledge in this chapter, as well as the amazing programmers out there who are kind enough to share some of these instruments for little to no cost. It starts with what synthesizers used to go for.

I got my first synthesizer at age 11. It was a Korg Poly-800, and I thought the world of it. It had around eight-voice polyphony, meaning you could essentially play eight keys at once before the notes would cut out on you.

It cost my parents $800 at the time—not a small amount of money even now. At the time, you would've thought that this amazing device would let me do everything—especially for $800. However, like all things electronic, once you invest in one device, you need another.

For Christmas the next year, I got a Roland TR-707 drum machine, along with a Vesta Fire 4-track. This probably cost around $1,000—not a cheap Christmas.

At that point, I really could create and produce the majority of my own music. However, next Christmas I realized that I could really use another synthesizer with another type of sound. And it never stopped....

Now, let's fast-forward to 2010. If I need the type of sound that a Poly-800 provides, I would be a bleeding idiot to go buy a plug-in that emulates it, because there are at least a hundred free plug-ins out there that have a very similar sound, and they don't cost a dime! Where's my $800?

It's still completely mind-boggling that what used to cost an exorbitant amount of money now costs nothing—if you know where to look. For that matter, if you just know how to do a Google search....

In this chapter, I'll spotlight some of my favorite freeware and competitively priced synthesizers. These are gems that I keep in my synth rack at all times, and believe me when I tell you that they have some personality. In fact, a couple of synthesizers listed here are very convincing emulations of what I used when I was 11. Perhaps that's why I listed them here.

## What Is a Synthesizer?

Let's make sure that you are up on what I'm talking about before we continue. I don't mean to condescend, but the word *synthesizer* isn't the friendliest term in the word for a newcomer. What does it mean?

Remember watching old Van Halen videos and seeing them start off a music video with a big piano-looking thing with knobs on it—a device similar to what you see in Figure 3.1?

These keyboard-controlled devices combine tones in interesting ways in an attempt to generate new sounds that can be played much like an organ or a piano.

**Figure 3.1** A classic synthesizer.

It is almost impossible to listen to a modern pop station and not hear a synthesizer-based sound during the first 15 minutes.

But what has taken synthesizers so far in music as we know it?

- Synthesizers can emulate the sounds of other instruments to a degree that might surprise you—especially with some of the modeling synthesizers that attempt to directly re-create the physics of a stringed instrument, and so on.

- Synthesizers can also be completely otherworldly, adding an atmosphere that no other instrument can bring to a project, such as alien landscapes, alien choirs, winds, and rain. They are good at making a picture in sound that will transport you.

- Synthesizers are also great for low end, leads, and filling in places that are completely missing in your song. Need a low, punchy bass and don't know a bass guitarist? Throw in a synth! Need a lead melody for that perfect hook, and the guitar isn't cutting it? Throw in a synth!

Many acts, such as Kraftwerk, shown in Figure 3.2, rely solely on synthesizers, with no other sounds added. The electronic tones take care of the whole song for them.

**Figure 3.2** Kraftwerk is a musical act based purely around synthesizers.

## Synthesizer Types

Despite the fact that most synthesizers tend to resemble one another, you may be surprised to know that they don't always work exactly the same; they use various methods of synthesis. And even when one synth uses the same form of synthesis as another, the two could still sound completely different due to their component makeup. For example, one synth may have two filters, while another synth has only one filter. It gets a lot deeper than that, though.

In this section, I'll go over a few of the different types of synthesis. However, keep in mind that these are only a few of them, and they tend to be the forms of synthesizers you'd most likely see available as shareware and so on.

## Subtractive Synthesis

The most common synthesizer type is the *subtractive* synthesizer. And for good reason—they are the easiest to program, and they provide the quickest results.

Moog synthesizers, as shown in Figure 3.3, are probably some of the most revered synths in terms of subtractive synthesizers. One big reason for the Moog praise is that their creator, whose name was Robert Moog, actually invented the synthesizer as we know it back in the day. If you don't believe me, look him up in the encyclopedia.

**Figure 3.3** The Moog synthesizer is still a very common sound in modern music, thanks to its inventor, Robert Moog.

The second big reason for the Moog praise is the giant, thick sound that these devices produce. To this day, I've never seen a computer-based synthesizer surpass the sound of a Moog synthesizer. However, it's fun to look and try!

But why are Moog synthesizers and all other synths that fall under the "subtractive" label described as subtractive? Essentially, these devices rely on filters to shape the overall tones, thus "subtracting" from the sound.

Think of how sculptors take a large block of clay and slowly cut from the block until it has shape and definition, as shown in Figure 3.4.

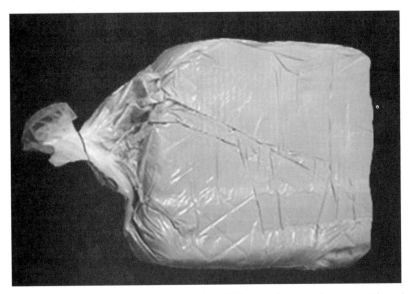

**Figure 3.4** Sculpting is a lot like subtractive synthesis. You take a large block and slowly cut away from it until you have the shape/sound you want.

Although this may sound complicated in theory, subtractive synthesizers actually represent the easiest to use of all synthesizers. You can just push buttons and turn knobs until you have what you want. And because of the quick results and ease of use, they make up the majority of synths listed in this chapter—and everywhere else.

## FM Synthesis

Were you one of the many cats in the '80s who loved the DX7, shown in Figure 3.5? This synthesizer was found onstage with many an artist: Herbie Hancock, Stevie Wonder, Steve Winwood, you name it.

**Figure 3.5** The Yamaha DX7 was a widely used synthesizer in the 1980s, though not the easiest to program.

Thankfully, whoever designed the preset sounds that existed within the DX7 did a good job, as there were very few people who were capable of understanding exactly how to program their own sounds with the DX7, given its small screen and difficult controls. But even if you had the large number of knobs and buttons that you'd need as opposed to the small data slider that was given, understanding FM synthesis would have been difficult.

FM synthesis actually works exactly the way that it's been named. FM stands for *frequency modulation*. One tone will modulate another, creating an altogether different sound. For example, I can take two tones: one a sawtooth and one a square wave. When I modulate the square wave with a sawtooth at a moderate speed, I create an entirely different tone.

This might sound like a very simple concept, but keep in mind that when you are working with several carriers and all of the havoc, realism, and noise that they can make, you are getting into some serious programming right there.

## Samplers

Samplers are without a doubt one of the biggest contributors to modern electronic music, modern theatrical music, and modern television music. See Figure 3.6 for a picture of a classic sampler, the Akai S950.

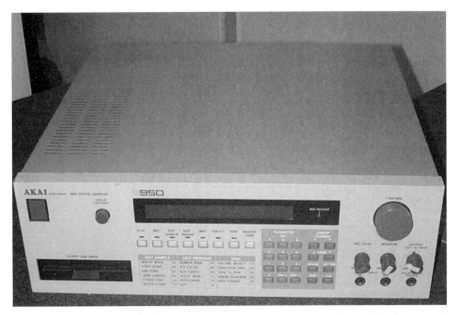

**Figure 3.6** The Akai S950, along with most other Akai samplers, was seen in studios across the country for years.

Although samplers aren't actually synthesizers in the truest sense, they do operate almost exactly the same, with two exceptions: what they use as an oscillator and the source of what they are synthesizing. For example, a synthesizer uses pure electronic tones. A sampler simply plays back a recorded audio file when you press a key. But where it gets interesting depends on which key of the keyboard you play, because a sampler pitches audio up and down based on which key you hit.

For example, if I play C3 on my keyboard controller, by default the sampler will play the audio file back at a normal speed. But if I play the key of C2, the same audio file will play back much more slowly. The reason why a sampler works this way is to allow you to make recorded audio essentially musical.

Another example, to give you a better idea, is this: If I recorded myself whistling in the key of C3 and then put this recording into a sampler, I could play the original key, and the whistle recording would play back normally. If I hit D3, the whistle recording would now play in D3, pitched slightly up.

Basically, the sampler plays back the recordings with normal keyboard tracking, like any synthesizer. You can even play chords of yourself whistling based on one audio recording. The only problem with a sampler is that the higher or lower key you press, the more unnatural the whistle will sound, because in the end it's just a slower version of a recording. There are ways to beat this limitation, however. If you are interested in learning more about samplers, look up "sampler" on Wikipedia—there's some great info there.

## Free Synthesizers

Now that we've gone through our primer, I'd like to take you through the true meat of the chapter—the free virtual synthesizers! These represent a list of worthy and stable plug-ins that have served me well. Don't let the "free" label dissuade you, by the way. I've used all of these plug-ins as readily as I would one that I'd purchased.

And remember, as I've mentioned in other chapters, if you like the product and you use it a lot, then donate! Many of the software developers that provide these plug-ins have PayPal access on their websites. You can donate whatever you feel you can, should, or want to. And with new funds at their disposal, maybe some of these excellent developers will provide us with another wonderful synthesizer to add beauty, depth, and thickness to our compositions.

## Togu Audio Line (PC and Mac)

If there is one developer out there that is at the top of my list, it's the Togu Audio Line (www.kunz.corrupt.ch). The talented and generous souls at TAL have provided not only a huge list of FX, EQs, and filters, which you can read more about in Chapters 4 and 5, but also a beautiful line of soft synthesizers.

One very important feature of most TAL products is that they support Mac and PC, VST and Audio Units.

So let's explore the synthesizers here!

### *TAL-Elek7ro*

The TAL-Elek7ro—or, if you aren't into the whole trendy hacker speak, TAL-Electro, is a very simple two-oscillator subtractive synthesizer (see Figure 3.7). However, its simplicity makes it quite advantageous.

**Figure 3.7** The TAL-Elek7ro is an amazingly robust soft synth with a very simple interface and a large sound.

It's incredibly easy to get those thick, deep basses, especially when you take advantage of the assignable LFOs. For example, you could assign one of the LFOs to the pulse-width modulation and get some extra thickness out of your sound. It's quite simple to get some very regal pads and some biting leads from the Elek7ro as well.

Unlike the other synths of the TAL line, the Elek7ro is an original creation that does not seek to emulate classic analog synths. Instead, it's a mixture of many different synths, akin to the Moogs and so on.

It can act as a polyphonic or a monophonic synth. This means you can play many keys simultaneously (polyphonic), or you can limit yourself to only being able to play one key at a time, like the classic synths (monophonic).

Another added benefit of the Elek7ro is that you may assign the LFOs to the FM modulation on either of the oscillators and use the Elek7ro as an FM synthesizer. However, it's nowhere near as complex as the DX7 we discussed earlier in this chapter.

All in all, I have a great time working with this synth, and it tends to come in the handiest when being used as a bass or a lead. Additionally, it's perfect for making percussion sounds. But don't let my usage of it dictate how you use it. Synths are made for experimentation, after all!

## TAL-U-No-62

These next two TAL soft synths are indeed my favorites—partially due to their nostalgia, but heavily due to their sound. The TAL-U-No-62 (see Figure 3.8) was my first discovery with TAL, and I have used it in my music for a long, long time. It's a beautiful re-creation of the Roland Juno-106, which I actually owned for several years. But you know how it is—with the emergence of the soft synth, I got rid of many pieces of gear. The TAL-U-No-62 made this easy! The Roland Juno-106 was heavy and bulky, and it tended to break down. The free soft synth version of it, shown in Figure 3.8, is quick, reliable, and still has that "sound."

**Figure 3.8**  The TAL-U-No-62 is a beautifully crafted nod to the Roland Juno-106.

I'd like to draw special attention to the Chorus I and Chorus II buttons. These chorus settings sound amazingly accurate compared to the original. They will truly thicken any sound that you are currently working on. And if you really like them, TAL also has a separate, free TAL-Chorus-60, also available at the TAL website.

**Figure 3.9**  The TAL-U-No-62 chorus sounds very similar to the original Juno-60 chorus, a defining feature of the classic synth.

Aside from the chorus, the synth boasts three basic oscillator waveforms (pulse, saw, and square) that can be used simultaneously (or not). There is one envelope that can be used for either the amplitude or the filter.

Speaking of filters, there is a dedicated low-pass filter and a dedicated high-pass filter. You can actually use both filters at once, allowing you to truly mold the sound you are looking for. For example, you can shelve a little bit of the high end off with the low-pass filter and then take a tiny bit of the low end off with the high-pass filter. This is great for those cool bass sounds that can sometimes interfere with your kick drum. In other words, you can get that good low-end bass sound with the low-pass filter and then shelve a little off with the high-pass so that you don't create some nasty mud in your mix.

In addition to basses, the TAL-U-No-62 excels at those warm pads that made the early Phil Collins/Genesis tracks so moody and interesting.

### TAL-BassLine

The TAL-BassLine, shown in Figure 3.10, is so much fun that you really should have to pay for it. It's a very accurate version of the SH-101 from Roland, with some cool additions that the original did not have.

**Figure 3.10** The TAL-BassLine is a wonderful emulation of the Roland SH-101.

For one thing, the TAL-BassLine has a very simple, very cool arpeggiator. Arpeggiators are great because you can easily come up with complex synth parts simply by holding down various notes at a time. Also, the BassLine has a Unison mode that the original did not have. This doubles the tone coming from the synthesizer, making it much thicker and much bigger.

With regard to how the BassLine is like the SH-101, the soft synth has three sources, or oscillators, or waveforms. These are the pulse wave, saw wave, and sine wave—again, like the U-No-62. In both cases, the sine wave acts as a sub, giving much-needed low end to the higher, "tinnier" waveforms.

Additionally, the BassLine has a standard low-pass filter that can be modulated by the envelope, and it has keyboard tracking and so on. To accompany the filter, there is a Warm Filter Feedback knob to give you more of an aggressive and vintage sound when using the BassLine.

If you're into vintage Roland synths, don't let this one pass you by, because it's dead on in many ways and is perfect for many different types of music.

## Synth1 by Ichiro Toda (PC Only)

The Clavia Nord Lead, shown in Figure 3.11, touched the lives of more than a few electronic musicians over the years, in many walks of music. It jumped onto the scene and stole the show within many

**Figure 3.11** The Nord Lead is an amazing synth that has had a major influence on many forms of music.

electro songs during the '90s. And the signature red chassis made it impossible to miss on stage.

Moving forward into the 2000s, the Nord Lead gained even more exposure as Top 40 acts such as the Killers made great use of the bright-red instrument within the studio and onstage.

Sometime during the rise of the Nord Lead, a very kind gentleman decided to see whether he could create a software emulation of it on his own time. Through careful programming and apparent love, he succeeded with a beautiful soft synth that closely emulates its estranged parent, the Nord Lead.

Synth1 (www.geocities.jp/daichi1969/softsynth/#down), as it is called, has basically all of the functionality of a Nord Lead 2, including:

- Four filter types
- An arpeggiator
- Two LFO types
- Tempo delay
- Light load on the processor
- A constantly growing preset library

Perhaps one of the greatest strengths of Synth1 (see Figure 3.12) is one that wasn't even intended. The online user base seriously latched on to this virtual instrument, and in doing so, they have gifted Synth1 with a huge library of presets created by the fans, for the fans, and for free.

Even if you are a Mac user or a Linux user, it may not hurt to salvage an old PC and trigger this synth remotely through MIDI, as it is well worth the effort.

**Note:** Keep in mind that the website for Synth1 is in Japanese; however, the download links are in English, and the synth is labeled in English, too.

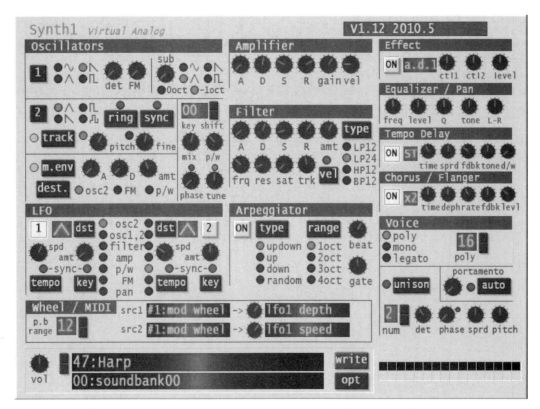

**Figure 3.12** Synth1 is an amazing free synth that closely emulates the Nord Lead 2.

## Hexter (Linux)

Just when you thought the chapter was going to be all about subtractive synthesizers, I throw in an FM synthesizer. Hexter (cutevst.sourceforge.net) is an FM synthesizer modeled off the DX7, mentioned earlier in this chapter.

Remember when I said the DX7 could be difficult to program? Hexter has made up for this by allowing all of the parameters it holds to be easily tweaked, as all software synthesizers should. See Figure 3.13.

If you have a real DX7, you'll be happy to know that Hexter can actually read DX7 SysEx files, so you can use your DX7 patches within Hexter.

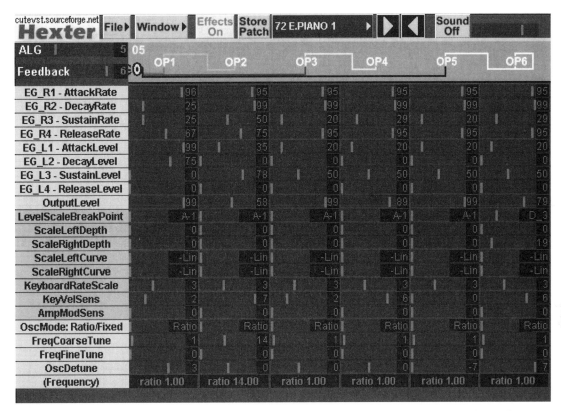

**Figure 3.13** Hexter is a fun FM synthesizer with a streamlined interface.

Also, Hexter, unlike the original DX7, includes its own FX, such as reverb, delay, chorus, and tube warmth.

Apparently, there was originally a Windows version of this synth; however, I was only able to access the Linux version. You may get lucky and find the Windows version floating around out there, though.

## Conclusion

This list of free synths is in no way intended to be the entire list of all of the free software synthesizers available. It is meant to be a showcase of synths that I've gotten good use out of and would recommend to any friend.

Although I definitely encourage you to investigate and try out the synthesizers listed in this chapter, I also encourage you to look for more synths for your arsenal. The electronic/computer-based music community is large and giving, and the people who make up the online body are constantly creating and inventing. Keep an eye out for what's new. Just remember to run a virus scan on things you download!

Also, remember that you can still use the synths listed in this chapter that do not support your current operating system. All you have to do is get your hands on an old PC or Mac, and you have an instant synth mule.

Also, for the Mac guys out there, keep in mind: Boot Camp, Fusion, Parallels! The PC emulators can assist you in adding several more synths that are not available for the Mac.

In the next chapter, get ready for some fun. We'll be looking at free FX!

**Interview with Ivan Cerrillo**

**Could you give us a quick introduction with some of the albums, software packages, and singles you've been a part of?**

My name is Ivan Cerrillo—an electronic-music fan, a DJ, and an amateur music composer. I have not yet participated in an album release simply because I've considered that the music I make is not commercial, and therefore it's not worth spending much money and effort to invest in whatever I end up composing.

**Is there a particular audio plug-in of which you are extremely fond? Feel free to list multiple ones.**

I've been creating my own music since 2005. For the same reason that I haven't taken myself too seriously, I've ended up trying all sorts of free VSTs and such. Among the ones I really like and would continue to use are Prodigious, Stringer, Carin Zodiac, and Ultrasoniq.

Other open-source audio plug-ins I've used include Audacity, MIDI Converter, Format Factory, and so on. There have been some plug-ins that have given me a headache—not just free, but even the ones I've had to pay for—so, in general, the difference between one another is very minimal. However, usually free ones are easier to install and work with.

As you can see, most of the plug-ins I've used are basic, and thus I've not released a record. The plug-ins have made it possible for fans to make decent music even if it's just for fun. Eventually, I may end up releasing a full album, but without making such a large investment, I can create, manipulate, and record whatever my mind is eager to compose at any given time.

# 4 FX

In the previous chapter we talked about instruments, and hopefully you are now in the process of playing and having fun with some of the instruments you downloaded. If that is the case, this is the perfect time to start talking about our next subject: FX.

Sure, the instruments are the cornerstones upon which all music is built, but FX give the instruments and audio tracks depth, dimension, thickness, and more.

Many of the DAW packages (refer to Chapter 2) that you can download for your audio/music-making needs will more than likely have FX available for you to use. These will range from mainstay FX, such as reverbs, to more esoteric FX, such as pattern-based filters and so on. However, I would also like to point out some other brilliant, free FX that will enhance your music-production experience!

If you're a veteran user, you might ask, "What makes one reverb or delay different from the rest? Why not just go with what is already in my DAW package?"

This is a compelling question. My answer is simply this: Like all things in this book, independent programmers tend to think outside of the box. This absolutely occurs with FX plug-ins. You may find a free reverb that absolutely blows away the one you use in Pro Tools, simply because someone thought outside of the box. Why not try some out?

First, let's take a look at one of the main effects used in music production: reverb.

# Reverb

Do most drums in the recordings you listen to sound as if they were recorded in a warm room with plenty of acoustic reinforcement, completely dry?

Well, parts of the drum kit—for example, the kick drum—will sound as if they were recorded in a dry location, but the snare usually tends to sound slightly hollow and have a little decay on it.

Vocals tend to sound as if they are a little wet as well. If you listen to a new Beyonce track (or whoever you are into), you'll notice there's a little tail on the end of the vocals. This is generally a reverb effect. It's necessary because completely dry sources of audio, such as vocals, drums, and so on, can sound dull in many cases. Reverbs add a nice little bit of ethereality and sparkle that makes certain parts of your mix stand out.

In a real-life scenario, you would achieve a reverb effect by placing someone in a tiled bathroom and then having him sing, play the snare drum, and so on. Reverb effects emulate the large tiled room and also allow you to control the overall wetness. Rather than having your recording subject sound as if he is recording in a bathroom, he can sound partially as if he is in a bathroom! But why is that a good thing?

Too much reverb on an audio source will make the subject sound washed out, dreary, and depressing. But if you add just a splash, you get a little bit of sparkle and depth on the back end. It's almost like adding a shadow to the drawing of a stick figure. A stick figure on its own looks like a boring little doodle. But if you add a shadow, somehow the stick figure seems more realistic and interesting.

So, in a sense, reverb is your shadow for audio!

In this section, I'd like to show you a few of the free reverb units that are out there waiting for you. Some of these are so pristine-sounding that you may mistake them for an old hardware unit, but you may be surprised by the performance.

## Nebula3 Free (PC and Mac, VST/AU)

Give a man an FX unit, and he has reverbs, phasers, mic emulations, and more for a day. Give a man a way to sample other FX units, and he has a lifetime of FX that will never grow old.

That is the mission of Nebula3 Free (www.acustica-audio.com; see Figure 4.1). Not only does it give you an amazing multi-FX unit (yes, it does more than reverbs), but also, on the PC end of things, it gives you a sampler that allows you to sample the FX algorithms of other FX devices and retain them within Nebula3 Free.

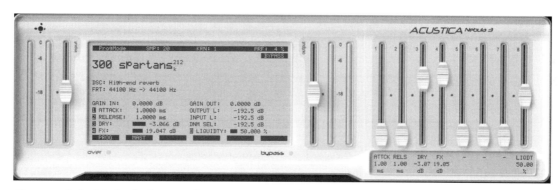

**Figure 4.1**   Nebula3 Free is an amazing freebie version of the larger Nebula3 proper.

Regrettably, the sampler does not come on the Mac version, but the FX on both the Mac and PC versions are sublime. If you are a PC user, by all means start sampling!

The reverbs sound warm and convincing, definitely reminiscent of the older Lexicon units from the '80s and '90s. The editing on Nebula3 is wonderful as well. All of the main parameters of the FX patches are mapped to handy sliders on the side of the unit.

I was seriously impressed by the phaser preset on Nebula3 as well. Aside from the reverbs, it gave convincing sweeps that reminded me much more of a hardware phaser (from which it was probably sampled) than any software effect I've heard thus far.

It took very little work to get Nebula3, so don't worry about forking over information and all that. All in all, this is definitely your first stop if you're looking for reverbs—and then some.

### TAL-Reverb III (PC and Mac, VST/AU) and TAL-Reverb II (PC, Mac, and Linux)

If you aren't much for complicated graphical reverb interfaces, do I have the plug-in for you! The TAL-Reverb III (kunz.corrupt.ch; see Figure 4.2) has a brilliantly streamlined interface that lets you just get rolling. Seriously, it has a total of seven sliders. How much easier can it get?

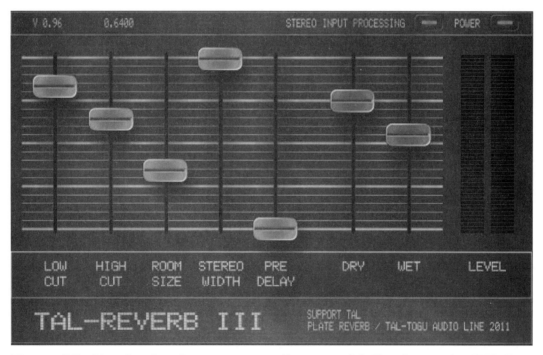

**Figure 4.2** Need a simple, great-sounding reverb? Check out the TAL-Reverb III (or II, if you are on Linux).

The reverb unit as a whole is meant to resemble a plate reverb, an old studio favorite that will never let you down. I've deployed and enjoyed this particular algorithm of reverb over the years for its clean quality that always adds some shimmer to vocals, drums, and even bass, if used correctly.

To start, you have thoughtful Low Cut and High Cut sliders to help moderate the mud in your performances. Moving on, you get the Room Size as a simple fader. Simply increase the fader and increase the overall "bigness" of the reverb. Just imagine the walls getting farther apart in your room.

Finally, there are the regular faders, such as Stereo Width, Dry, and Wet. These simply let you modify how spread out the reverb is, how reverb-y the track as a whole is, and how much of the dry track is allowed through. You are also able to choose whether you want the reverb to process your signal in stereo or mono.

The TAL-Reverb in all of its incarnations is light on the presets; a total of 10 ship with it. The unit is really easy, though. In fact, it's easy enough for you to create many, many presets. No complaint there.

If you are a Linux user, a link has been posted on the main webpage, stating that many of the TAL plug-ins have now been ported over to Linux to be a part of KXStudio.

---

**Note:** KXStudio is a GNU/Linux operating system, based on Ubuntu, for artists, producers, musicians, and so on. The greatest part about it is that it's free and includes support for music applications such as Ardour, which also support the VST plug-in. KXStudio comes with a slew of plug-ins beyond just this small reverb that will simply bring a tear to your eye.

Whether you are a Mac or PC user, you should check out KXStudio; it may change you.

---

## Chorus/Flange

When you listen to vocals on one of your favorite CDs, do you ever notice how they may sound thicker, wider, and just a little larger than life? Chorus is one effect that really will do that for you.

Chorus works by doubling the signal coming in and then slightly detuning it. When you play the dry signal and the detuned signal together, you get a much thicker sound in general.

Flange is very similar, but it is an identical signal that it slightly delayed. Because the signals are so close, you can get a sweeping effect that can be strengthened or decreased by changing the delay between the signals.

Chorus and flange are great for many different applications. Beef up certain sections of your drums, bass guitars, and vocals. These are versatile effects that you can apply in large or small amounts, depending on what you're going for. Be careful about using too much on vocals, though—you can get a serious nasal quality in your vocals if you do.

In this section, we'll take a look at some chorus/flange plug-ins and see what's out there.

## MonstaChorus (PC and Mac, VST/AU)

Everyone has this idea that the more complex the plug-in is, the bigger it's going to sound. This was never true in hardware, though, and it's definitely not the case when it comes to MonstaChorus from Betabugs Audio (www.betabugsaudio.com; see Figure 4.3).

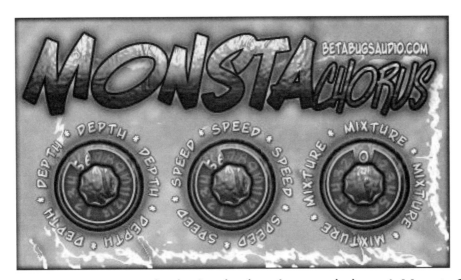

**Figure 4.3** It may look simple, but it sounds huge! MonstaChorus makes things sound big.

There are just three knobs on MonstaChorus:

- **Depth.** Determines how intense the modulation is.

- **Speed.** Controls the speed of the modulation.

- **Mixture.** Determines how much of the overall effect you hear as opposed to how much dry signal you hear.

The concept is very simple, very plain, and doesn't leave much to the imagination. But the sound gets very large. I've found that seriously increasing the depth and speed gives vocals a really great alien/demon effect for having fun. I've also found that for normal usage, MonstaChorus has simply made my vocals smoother and more epic. It's a wonderful effect, really.

## Blue Cat's Stereo Flanger (PC and Mac, VST/AU/DX)

The flange effect was at its most popular during the '70s and '80s. Many a bass guitar could be heard thumping away, running through a flange pedal, and many a keyboard could be heard running through the flange setting on a MidiVerb3. Blue Cat Audio (www.bluecataudio.com) brings you a classic re-creation of a true bit of yesteryear for nothing at all.

The Blue Cat Stereo Flanger (see Figure 4.4) can go from being a very mild, warming effect to being an intense, spacey sound immersion with very little effort. It gives you the classic Delay, Depth, and Rate controls that you'll be used to after you work with this particular type of plug-in for a while.

What's interesting is that the Stereo Flanger gives you control over the forward modulation and the backward modulation of the flange as well. This really lets you customize each setting—especially because they've made the waveform of your modulation available as well.

There are several versions of Blue Cat's Stereo Flanger available, which is rare for free plug-ins; it even runs in 64-bit. Also, the guys at Blue Cat were nice enough to include a stereo and a mono version of the flanger.

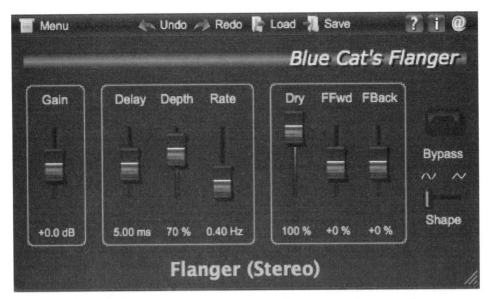

**Figure 4.4** Bring back the '80s with Blue Cat's Stereo Flanger.

I will note that you can, in fact, re-create the old '80s synth bass very easily with the Stereo Flanger and any punchy little synth bass you can find at your disposal. So, if there are any Human League fans out there, you're going to be excited.

## Delay/Echo

You know those cool moments in certain songs when all the music cuts off, and suddenly you just hear the voices echoing, almost in the distance?

Delay, also known as *echo*, has multiple purposes. From filling up empty space to being an instrument unto itself for some musicians (the Edge from U2, would be a good example), delay is a must!

For many people, simply having an echo is enough, regardless of the specific settings. For some, though (especially those who use it instrumentally), the additional settings—namely the time of the delay—are what makes the echo so intrinsic to their music.

The ability to sync the delay to the host clocks of various audio applications has been a wonderful feature in delay modules since computer audio plug-ins became prevalent. Gone are the days of having to turn the Delay Time knob until the delay speed matches the audio speed that is going into it, such as guitar strums and so on. Using the sync feature, you can have the delay automatically match up with the BPM at which your song is record. You just choose the note value, such as eighth notes.

In this section, we'll take a look at some of the delay/echo modules out there.

## TAL-DUB-III (PC, Mac, and Linux, VST/AU)

There really couldn't be a more perfect example of a delay unit for this section beyond what the TAL-DUB-III (kunz.corrupt.ch; see Figure 4.5) has to offer. It's simple, it's elegant, and it sounds great.

**Figure 4.5** Echo your heart out with the TAL-DUB-III.

This plug-in does not attempt to reinvent anything; it simply does what it says it will do—creates a dub-style delay with its own sound. It does not attempt to re-create the tape delays of old within this particular plug-in (though TAL does have a plug-in that does this); it just works as a good ol' workhorse delay plug. Period.

In the true dub tradition, the TAL-DUB-III gives you a very long four-second delay time that ultimately will give you a nice, crude, looping delay, should you choose to use it that way. You can also sync it to your host clock, and it offers a large array of quantized settings for your choosing.

Additionally, you are provided with a ×2 button per stereo channel, which doubles the amount of delay coming from the unit. I particularly enjoy the sound of this setting for melodic/arpeggiated parts.

And it has so much more for such a small delay unit! One lovely feature is the Tab button that allows you to tap tempo your delay. There is MIDI Learn as well, so you can assign a MIDI controller directly to TAL-DUB-III.

If there ever were a developer deserving of your PayPal donation, this would be the one. And as mentioned, this plug-in is for all platforms. So run for this one; don't walk!

## KR-Delay FS (PC and Mac, VST/AU)

I'll admit it; I have a thing for plug-ins that look as cool as they sound. The KR-Delay FS (www.kresearch.com/Free-Series.htm; see Figure 4.6) is exactly that—a cool-sounding, cool-looking delay plug-in that shows you graphically what it's doing, while also letting you hear it.

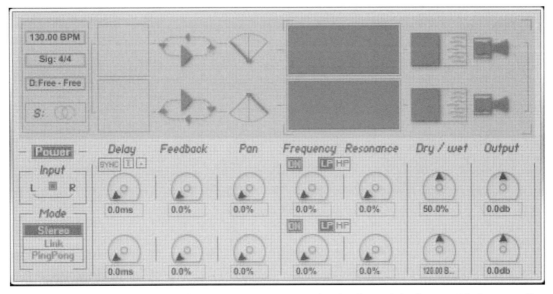

**Figure 4.6** Beautiful-looking programs gel nicely with beautiful-sounding plug-ins, especially where KR-Delay FS is concerned.

Similar to TAL-DUB-III, KR-Delay FS is a stereo delay with a high- and low-pass filter to help you avoid muddy, echo-y mixes that belong in a toilet.

What's so neat is that it actually shows you, with a graphic representation, where frequencies are being cut, what the feedback is doing, where the panning is going on, and what channel is louder than another. This is perfect for an enthusiast who isn't really acquainted with how a signal flow works within an echo device.

KR-Delay FS also can be synced and gives you a wide range of possibilities for how it's synced. And, you can switch it from stereo mode over to ping-pong mode, which takes greater advantage of the stereo possibilities available within KR-Delay FS. For example, you can have it echo once in one speaker, then again in another speaker automatically, using the ping-pong effect.

The only thing somewhat annoying about this plug-in is that it's entirely in grayscale. This makes some of the buttons hard to see. Once you're used to it, though, it's a lot of fun to learn and hear.

## Compressor/Limiter

There is one effect that actually doubles more as sonic tool; it helps you sculpt a sound, much like an equalizer does.

Compression is a must-have tool for any artist willing to try his hand in audio production. It makes drums more present and makes extremely energetic artists...um, less dynamic. In other words, if you have a friend who sings, and he is really loud one minute and really soft the next, making your engineering experience a nightmare, then you need a compressor!

Compressors are meant to squash the dynamics in audio so that they sit in the mix easier, period. But you can also use them to squash down a mix to a steady stream of volume, so that when the gain is raised on the track, you have one very loud mix. This has become very, very common in modern music recording, much to the dismay of some.

In the audio world, compressors and limiters are very much like peanut butter and jelly. In fact, they go together so beautifully that there are many plug-ins and hardware modules that are, in fact, "compressor/limiters"—both functions are built in together. The compressor squashes the lows and the highs, while the limiter makes sure that the boosted signal never goes past a certain level.

Let's take a look at a couple of really amazing compressors. In fact, I'm still shocked these are free!

## CamelCrusher (PC and Mac, VST/AU)

People like thick, dirty drums. Hip-hop, R&B, dubstep, rock, grunge, and more have all proved it. In fact, most of us like dirt in general, stirred slightly with some low end and a bit of groove.

CamelCrusher from Camel Audio (www.camelaudio.com; see Figure 4.7) is the missing element for that, and many artists have discovered this time and time again—not just with CamelCrusher, but with all of the other fine products that are made over at Camel Audio. Take a look at some of the musicians who endorse the stuff, and I'm sure your curiosity will be piqued.

So what is all the fuss about? CamelCrusher is a free version of Camel-Phat from Camel Audio. Whereas CamelPhat is a multi-FX unit, CamelCrusher is only a compressor, distortion unit, and filter.

I'd like to bring your attention specifically to the compressor. It has a Phat mode that adds a bit of an overdrive, which, of course, you can disable. Other than that, it's just a knob for more compression, even more compression, and a ton of compression.

When I run drums through it, they get big, bigger, and huge. The compressor on CamelCrusher instantly gives that thickness that we listen for in all of our favorite tracks.

It's also good for bass, guitar, and more. CamelCrusher gives instant character that a lot of us end up spending hours on with multiple plug-ins.

**Figure 4.7** Beat the hell out of your audio and make it love you with the CamelCrusher.

What's also neat about CamelCrusher is that, like its big brother, CamelPhat, CamelCrusher has a Randomize button. If the sound isn't quite what you're looking for, hit the Randomize button until you get something you like.

Also, if you right-click on any of the knobs, you can select MIDI Learn and select Linear and Circular for the knob behaviors.

The presets that come with CamelCrusher are few, but they are more than adequate. Each one seems to fill a niche for any situation. But if you want to come up with your own, it never hurts.

## W1 Limiter (PC and Mac, AU/VST)

One of the most famous software limiters out there (and it has been for years) is the L1 Limiter from Waves. You will find this plug-in at every studio, production house, mastering studio, and more. It's a simple plug-in that does its job well. It just limits.

Some time back, George Yohng, a do-it yourselfer with a giving spirit, decided he'd rather not spend the exorbitant amount of money that the Waves bundle costs. At the time, you had to buy the bundle to get the L1, and it wasn't cheap. Look it up!

He decided to make his own L1, which he called the W1 (www.yohng.com/w1limit.html; see Figure 4.8). And as someone who has used the L1 a lot, I can attest that the W1 comes very, very, very close. In fact, it comes close enough that I don't really care. I'll go with free!

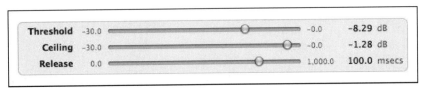

**Figure 4.8**  Why pay hundreds for an L1 Limiter when you can get the W1?

Like the L1, the W1's controls are simple. There's a Threshold slider, a Ceiling slider, and a Release slider. Adjust the threshold to the appropriate signal for what you have incoming, adjust the ceiling to the maximum possible volume coming out, and adjust the release where needed. That part always depends on what you have coming in.

Bottom line: Nothing gets past this thing. When it's attenuated, it's attenuated. That's the end of the story. True brickwall limiting.

So, if you're a Waves owner who regularly uses the L1, I invite you to compare. If you're a wannabe Waves owner, get the W1!

## Conclusion

At this point, we have seen many effects—enough to give you all of the mainstay effects for any production you may have coming up. By no means are these all the ones out there, but I guarantee you will enjoy them.

**Interview with Joe Virus**

**Could you give us a quick introduction with some of the albums, software packages, and singles you've been a part of?**

I'm Joe Gonzales. I am a DJ/VJ, remixer, musician, and producer. I write under the name Joe Virus. I have a few musical projects for which I write and perform. Solemn Assembly is a synth-pop and industrial band, Notify 9×9 is my dark dub project, and Program 88 is an '80s-inspired electro-pop band. I have done several remixes, including a remix of a track called "Assumptions" on Sinsect's *Shadow Wars* E.P. and a remix of the song "Grace" on Soil & Eclipse's *Grace* E.P. I have also independently remixed many of the tracks in my DJ sets. I have written and produced all of the releases by Solemn Assembly, Program 88, ChUcKY ChERnOByL, and Notify 9×9.

**How much experience have you had with free or open-source music plug-ins?**

I have used several free plug-ins in most of my work for the past 10 years, both synths and effects. I was tied down to hardware since the late '80s, drowning in MIDI cables and power strips, so I was looking into streamlining the studio. My friend, Richard Tull, helped me put together my first music PC in 2001, but after it was built, I was really turned off by how much I had to pay for software to do what I was already doing with my hardware synths and effects. I think for my first DAW, I paid around $300, and it was a "lite" version with minimal VSTs. Someone told me about a magazine that had freeware synths and effects, and I started my search for more. Now I have a wide array of freeware instruments and effects.

**Is there a particular audio plug-in of which you are extremely fond? Feel free to list multiple ones.**

Kieran Foster's Glitch has been my favorite audio tweaker plug-in for quite a while now. It is like a step sequencer for effects that can manipulate audio in ways that used to take me hours to do in other programs. I use it on everything from drum loops to vocals. It has a cool TapeStop effect that you can speed up or slow down, which is really awesome for breakdowns and transitions in some of my tracks. The Retrigger function is great for my synth build-ups, repeating the note like a drum roll. The Gater function is an automated gate for which you can change the speed, length, and volume, which comes in handy when I want some tempo-synced gated vocals or synths. It also has a Modulator, Shuffler, Crusher, Delay, and Stretcher, as well as controls for overdrive, master filter, step envelope, and a de-clicker. I have probably overused this plug-in at times, but I still turn to it for most of my projects. The great part about Glitch is how much control you have over each parameter.

**Could you share a quick story about where this plug-in has really shined during your music creation/production work?**

When I first stumbled upon Glitch, I was writing new tracks every day, using it in outrageous and over-the-top ways, creating very tweaked-out and disjointed tracks that I released under the name ChUcKY ChERnOByL. It was borderline Drum & Bass / IDM. It was a fun project, and I would tweak out every part of the tracks in Glitch, and then I would run the whole mix through Glitch to make it more extreme! But when I started working on the Notify 9×9 project, it was more down-tempo and dubby than the ChUcKY ChERnOByL music. It was very dark and moody, and I realized that if I used Glitch in a more subtle way, it could add to the depth and atmosphere of the sound. I started using it only on one or two parts, like a hi-hat loop or a mechanical gear sound, and it really made a bigger impact than using it on everything. So Glitch has been a staple in the Notify 9×9 arsenal of plug-ins.

**Is there a particular free/open-source virtual instrument of which you've become fond? Feel free to list multiple ones.**

I really love all of my synths from Togu Audio Line. The TAL Elek7ro synth is great! It has two oscillators on which you can select waveforms, a sub-oscillator, and two LFOs that are assignable to the filter, oscillators, pulse width, panning, or volume. It just sounds raw when I'm using it in my tracks. For a track I wrote for Notify 9×9, I assigned the LFO 1 to the cutoff of the filter using a triangle waveform and syncing it to the tempo at 2/1 to get a nice filter sweep over the pattern. I use LFO 2 assigned to the OSC 2 (pulse wave) using a triangle waveform and syncing it to the tempo at 1/2 to tweak it out. Automating my adjusting of the envelopes in the DAW gives the sound a live feel. I also suggest checking out the TAL NoiseMaker synth. Besides having two oscillators, it has an envelope editor that allows you to draw the envelope and assign it to the filter, the oscillators, the FM amount, the ring modulation, or the volume and lets you adjust the speed up to ×32.

**Could you share a quick story about where this instrument has really shined during your music creation/production work?**

I wrote a track for Solemn Assembly called "Aftershock" on my guitar and wanted to put a big-sounding bass line behind it, but all of my bass sounds were too "synthy," and it didn't mix well with the guitars. So I opened up

TAL Elek7ro and started working on making a big, booming bass. I started out with OSC 1 using a pulse waveform and OSC 2 using a sawtooth waveform. I also turned the sub-OSC to a square waveform. Instead of a bass synth sound, it had a bit of a bell tone. I started adjusting all of the parameters, and all of a sudden this dark and nasty-sounding digital gong sound came out, and I knew that was what I needed! I saved it as the Aftershock synth and a big reverb to it, put it in the mix, and it really made the song happen. Sometimes the best sounds come out of nowhere or from little mistakes you make. This was huge, and I definitely owe the song's power to the TAL Elek7ro.

**Have you had any difficulties installing or working with any of the free/open-source plug-ins that you've checked out?**

I really haven't had any problems with any freeware yet. I had my DAW crash a few times due to an overload of plug-ins, but that was just me pushing the limits of my computer's memory. Most of the plug-ins I use are fairly easy to install, and especially now, using a Mac, it is easy to drop the AU components into the folder and go!

**Do you have any advice for beginner musicians/ producers working with free/open-source audio plug-ins?**

Try as many freeware plug-ins as you can find! There are really great-sounding free synths out there and great effects that I haven't even begun to touch on. Look online for user groups and chat rooms that deal with plug-ins, and you'll definitely find some great tools to work with. I typed "free audio plug-ins" into my search engine online and came up with several places to download them. And don't forget about the magazines— go to your local bookstore and look through their music magazine section, and you should find some awesome resources there.

Remember that sometimes less is more and that with all the free plug-ins available, you don't need to use the same effect chains over and over. And sometimes making mistakes in your editing can be a good thing.

There are so many tools available for free that you have no excuse for not making the music you always wanted to make.

# 5 Drum Machines

Of all the different instruments being combined to make modern music, drums are the only common denominator. Not every song has guitar, and not every song has keyboards, but all songs have drums—even classical pieces. Triangles and timpani drums are percussion, right?

You need drums! Plain and simple, they help drive the music you create, they provide rhythm, and they are a heck of a lot of fun!

In this chapter, we'll explore drum plug-ins that can give you the palette of raw percussive power that you've craved since you were a child, tapping on your desk.

As per the norm with this book, the goal is to show you good, powerful, and free/cheap drum plug-ins that not only will rock your world, but also will give you the power you long for.

## Sample-Based Drum Plug-Ins

The most common form of drum plug-in you will encounter is a particular type of drum module that uses audio files, or *samples*, for each particular drum sound it provides.

What will generally happen is, after you've installed the drum plug-in and launched it in your host application (refer to Chapter 2 on DAWs), the drum plug-in will appear in your DAW. Because this plug-in will be instantiated as an instrument, you most likely will trigger it with your MIDI controller, if you have one.

When triggering a drum plug-in via MIDI, always start from C1 on your MIDI controller. This has been the norm for drum modules, hardware drum machines, and so on as far back as the '80s, with General MIDI and such. The kick is usually mapped to C1, the snare is set to D1, and so on.

The first time you trigger one of the sample-based drum plug-ins, you'll notice that the drums will sound real, for the most part. This is because the sounds being triggered are actually recorded drum sounds. Press C1, and a recording is triggered of an actual bass drum recording. It will be only one quick instant of the kick drum's recording, giving you a single note, but it's a recording nonetheless. Some plug-ins will even let you change out drum sounds of your own.

In this first section, we'll take a look at some of the drum plug-ins that use audio files to create sounds.

## DrumCore Free (PC and Mac)

DrumCore (www.sonomawireworks.com; see Figure 5.1) offers one of the most incredibly robust free plug-ins I have ever heard of. But before I move into why it's astounding that you get so much, let me explain what DrumCore is.

At its heart, DrumCore is a drum playback plug-in that not only allows you to trigger individual drum sounds via a MIDI controller, but also allows you to choose from several MIDI drum loops or audio drum loops. You can simply drag these loops into your host application (such as REAPER, Ardour, or GarageBand).

The loops and kits come from well-known professionals and even include a picture of the person who made the kit.

What's so incredible is that the free version of DrumCore does not limit you in any way with its usage. It's missing some of the bigger features of the full version, but the features that are around are still plenty for most of us.

**Figure 5.1** DrumCore Free is an extensive and giant-sounding drum player and loop player. It's hard to believe it's free!

For example, you get:

- One electronic and one acoustic drum kit. These are not small kits, either. There are several sections within each kit.

- More than a hundred audio loops.

- More than a hundred MIDI loops.

And later, you always have the option of purchasing different kits if you decide you want more.

I was stunned by how lifelike and big both kits were. I really can't believe they're free!

One thing to note is that DrumCore Free is a really big download (around 600 MB). You can download directly from the Sonoma Wire Works website, or you can just download the torrent.

## MDrummer Small (PC and Mac)

MeldaProduction also offers an amazing version of their popular MDrummer drum plug-in (www.meldaproduction.com; see Figure 5.2). Known simply as MDrummer Small, it gives you a large number of very cool drum loops.

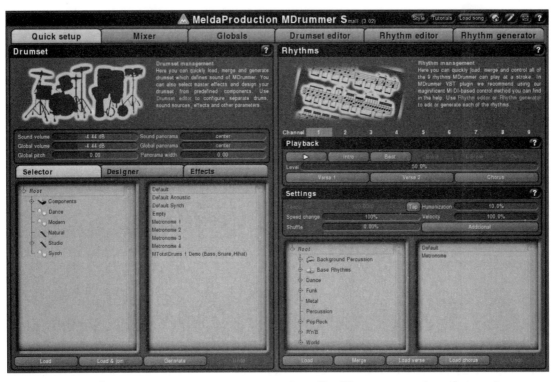

**Figure 5.2** Like DrumCore, MDrummer Small offers a couple of very impressive kits and loops that are free for you to use within any project you currently have going.

Like DrumCore, which I mentioned in the previous section, it's almost frightening that they give away kits of this quality. Realistically, the acoustic kit alone could easily work for your entire album, because it's dialed in and just crazy authentic. But they go a step farther by letting you use a stripped-down version of their very cool drum sequencer.

Within said sequencer, there are specific buttons for breaks, intro, outro, verse, and chorus—standard stuff that we all expect. You can use the buttons to trigger different parts or just to demo the kit.

If you play your MIDI controller on the default MIDI channel of MDrummer, you'll actually be triggering loops sequentially, part to part. However, if you trigger MDrummer with MIDI Channel 10, then you can trigger individual drum parts, such as the kick on C1, snare on D1, and so on.

Another important feature disabled in MDrummer Small is the Mixer. However, you can disable individual drum parts, which allows you to track individual drums to different audio tracks.

Within MDrummer, you will find a button toward the top called Tutorials, which guides you to a website with extensive videos explaining MDrummer's usage in different DAWs and so on.

All in all, I highly recommend MDrummer, as it really does sound as if a kit is in the room with you, and it's sure to have colleagues asking whether you used a real drummer on that song.

## SampleTank FREE (PC and Mac)

Generally, when you think of SampleTank, drums don't come to mind. But SampleTank has a lot of drums—and everything else. Another startling thing about SampleTank FREE (www.ikmultimedia.com; see Figure 5.3) is the fact that they give you so many sounds with a free piece of software.

SampleTank FREE consists of a 500-MB sample library filled with pads, basses, guitars, loops, and, most importantly, drums. Because it's also a 16-part multitimbral sample device, you can run many tracks off of one instantiation of SampleTank FREE, allowing you to conserve resources.

**Figure 5.3** SampleTank FREE provides tons of drum patches and more for absolutely nothing. But it's a huge download!

IK Multimedia requires you to jump through a few hoops to get SampleTank FREE. You'll need to set up an account with their website and so on. It's really not a lot to ask for given how much you get, though. However, there is a lot to download with this plug-in—it's huge, in terms of size—so get ready! But the end result was worth it.

The drum and synth patches are very well polished and are worthy additions to any project.

I have to say that out of all of the free sample players available, SampleTank FREE is by far the most generous. Check it out!

## LinuxSampler (PC, Mac, and Linux, AU/VST/DSSI/LV2)

The LinuxSampler project is an amazing feat stemming from an amazing goal:

> "...to produce a free, streaming capable open source pure software audio sampler with professional grade features, comparable to both hardware and commercial Windows/Mac software samplers and to introduce new features not yet available by any other sampler in the world."

**Figure 5.4** LinuxSampler is an ambitious project that is continually growing.

No small task there, huh? Well, they did accomplish it, and LinuxSampler (www.linuxsampler.org; see Figure 5.4) boasts a very robust feature list that is still growing.

But wait—what does this have to do with drums? If you flip back through the pages of this chapter and look at the drum playback devices already listed, keep one thing in mind: They are samplers as well. In fact, they are samplers with drum patches preloaded. They are also samplers that are just like LinuxSampler—they are just configured for drummers.

LinuxSampler does everything listed earlier; you just have to create your own drum patches or find sample libraries supported by Linux-Sampler, which currently are Giga 1 and Giga 2 sample libraries.

If you're familiar with the Giga format, you'll know that it originated from Tascam's now-defunct GigaSampler line of software. This is sad for Tascam but wonderful for you because at one time these were some of the best-sounding sample libraries on the market. And, what's even better is the simple fact that these sample libraries are still around and getting cheaper by the day. These libraries include amazing drum kits, amazing orchestral expansions, and more. LinuxSampler.org even has some of these libraries available for you to download right now—for free.

Of equal interest is the wonderful fact that LinuxSampler also supports the Akai S1000/S3000 formats. These samplers were the bee's knees back in the day, and they have extensive libraries—libraries, I might add, that have been very much a part of mainstream music for the past two decades.

Beyond just being a cool sample project, however, LinuxSampler is a constantly growing project with ambitious plans. These plans include:

- MIDI over Ethernet
- Audio over Ethernet
- Gig v3 sampler convolution-reverb presets
- Open sound control
- Network cluster support

Whew! These are all the features of the big software samplers. This is open source?!

---

**ReBirth**    ReBirth by Propellerhead (see Figure 5.5) is now a free (yet unsupported) software application that sports two very cool step-sequenced drum machines. These drum machines closely emulate the Roland TR-808 and TR-909. Also, if you're a Reason fan (also by Propellerhead, but not free), Reason still sports the ReBirth device, allowing you to run ReBirth along with Reason.

It's also possible to sync ReBirth with other software applications, such as Cubase. For Mac users, it's important to note that ReBirth only runs in the Mac Classic environment. So, if you're running Leopard, Snow Leopard, and so on, it won't work. Get yourself Parallels, Boot Camp your machine, or find an old Mac.

**Figure 5.5** Although ReBirth isn't just a drum machine, it's still free and tons of fun.

# Synth-Based Drum Machines

In the previous section, we looked at sample playback devices that focused on drums, and in some cases, other sounds. In this section we're going to cover another type of drum module that utilizes a synthesizer engine for producing percussive sounds.

As explained earlier, the aforementioned devices use actual recorded drum sounds that can be triggered via MIDI. Synth-based drum machines use oscillators, filters, LFOs, and envelopes instead.

Generally, you'll start off with either a sine wave or white noise, and you'll mold a sound with the envelopes and filters to make the sound either start abruptly or fade in. You can also use LFO (*low-frequency oscillator*) modulation to make the sound more complex. Essentially, you'll use the LFO to bend sound either slowly or rapidly. There are numerous combinations, and tons of electro sounds are possible. In some cases, realistic sounds are possible, too—if you're clever.

As you may have gathered by this point, synth-based drum machines are re-creations of older drum machines, such as the Roland 909, 808, and so on, that are not meant to sound real. In fact, they flaunt their artificiality in playful ways, making them ideal for electronic-oriented music.

It is possible to make these plug-ins sound more realistic through the use of effects such as reverbs. A reverb simulates a space, which is precisely what an electronic sound needs to sound realistic, as it has actually been generated in an electronic environment. Once an electronic sound sits in a room, an electronic cowbell, for example, suddenly sounds as if it is actually metallic.

If you are an artist who tends to focus on realistic, I caution you to still give these plug-ins a chance—you may be able to simulate percussive devices for which you don't currently have a recording—and learn something new! Sample playback devices rely on drum recordings for realism. Synth-based drum devices let you make full-on drum sounds of your own from scratch!

## MiniSpillage (Mac, AU)

MiniSpillage (www.audiospillage.com; see Figure 5.6) is the little brother to AudioSpillage's DrumSpillage drum synthesizer. Although seriously streamlined from the parent plug-in, MiniSpillage is still quite usable in its own right.

Although it only allows three percussive sounds at a time, it is quite easy to instantiate MiniSpillage many times within a project, as it does not use much of your CPU's processing power. This is actually ideal for many recording engineers, because having each drum on a different track is always the best way to go, yet some of the more hardcore drum

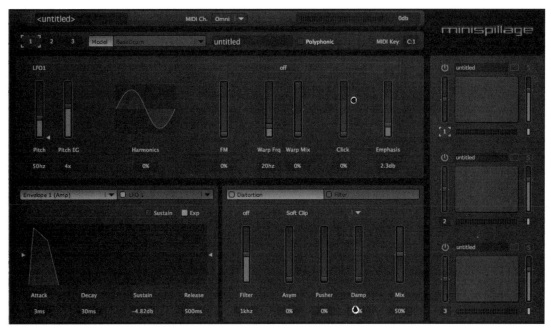

**Figure 5.6** MiniSpillage is an amazing, simple synthesized drum AU plug-in with a deep sound, and it's light on the processor.

samplers make this impossible due to the extensive resources they use in one instantiation.

On the sound edge of things, MiniSpillage offers an extremely clean sound with lots of low end and shimmer. It comes stock with several presets that are very much ideal for dance music, hip-hop, R&B, retro, and so on.

The interface is extremely user-friendly and makes it fun and easy for newcomers to synthesis to start making their own sounds.

You start off one of three models available within MiniSpillage. Each model has the appropriate parameters for the drums you are trying to create. For example, the bass drum model has different parameters from the wood drum model, and so on. The click slider is for the high-end tap part when a beater hits the bass drum.

MiniSpillage also allows you to save your own drum sounds that you create. This is a wonderful way to build your own custom drum library over time.

All in all, MiniSpillage is a very simple introduction to drum synthesis, completely for free. Yes, you can only use three drums per instantiation, but as mentioned earlier, it's light on the CPU, so you can load it up several times for a full kit.

## KickMaker (PC and Mac, VST/AU)

For a long, long time I was a do-it-yourselfer when it came to drum sounds. I was not content to load up a patch from Reason, Logic, or Pro Tools—I wanted to make *my own* drums. If you fall into this category, you really should check out KickMaker from Teragon Audio (www.teragonaudio.com; see Figure 5.7).

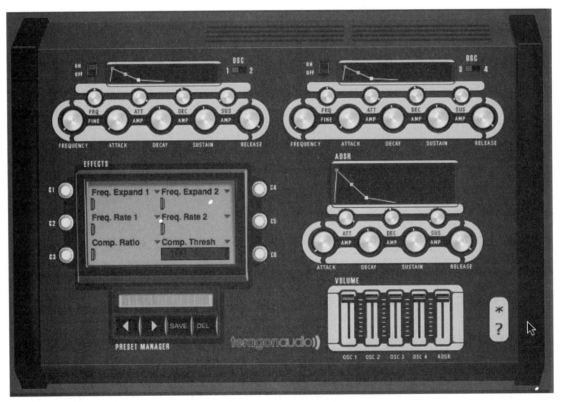

**Figure 5.7** Like big kick drums? Check out KickMaker!

KickMaker gives you the fun ability to explore synthesis aimed squarely at what the name implies—building kick drums. These kicks are not geared toward acoustic sounds in a modeling sense; they are geared toward dance music, hip-hop, electro, R&B, house, and so on.

The beef of KickMaker comes from its four oscillators, which can be individually sculpted between two frequency envelopes and one global envelope. (The two frequency envelopes will individually switch between covering all four oscillators, so there are actually four envelopes in addition to the global envelope.)

You are also provided with an extremely comprehensive effects section that houses access to additional settings, such as phase, filter settings, compressor settings, and even additional waveforms for the individual oscillators.

Finally, the volume section lets you control the overall volume of each oscillator and the ADSR envelope.

KickMaker comes with a healthy supply of presets; however, I'd like to say that the presets do not appear to really show off what KickMaker is actually capable of. With that being said, I implore you to download KickMaker and run it through the paces!

## Grizzly (PC, VST)

There are many VST drum modules out there. There are many different shapes, sizes, functions, and so on. The more elaborate drum modules tend to cost money—especially drum VSTs that have extensive MIDI capabilities and so on.

Enter Grizzly, the product of a VST developer contest. Grizzly (http://www.majken.se; see Figure 5.8) gives you features that tend to appear only in the products you have to pay for. For example, there are built-in effects, remapping capabilities, up to eight drum samples, and more.

Technically, Grizzly belongs in the earlier section, as it is a sample-playback module. I opted to place it here, though, because it resembles older analog drum modules.

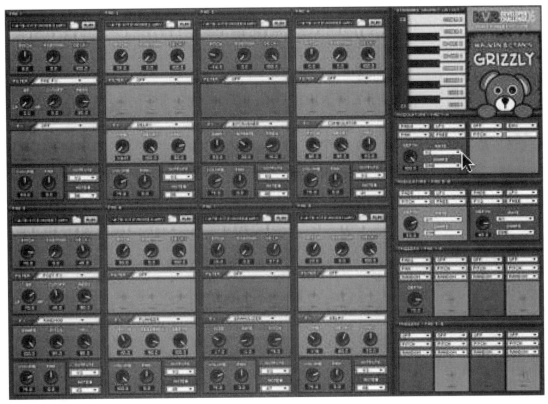

**Figure 5.8** Rock out with an analog-looking drum module, for free, with a feature set very similar to Native Instruments' Battery.

If you're familiar with Battery, by Native Instruments, you'll be extremely impressed by Grizzly, as the feature set and GUI are very similar.

Sadly, Grizzly is only for the PC, and you'll have to deal with a few bugs. The main one is that with your first install on a clean PC, the Grizzly font may not show up, making the loaded sound-file titles look like gibberish. If you reinstall, this fixes the issue.

In closing, I'd like to reiterate that the Grizzly VST is very extensive for a free plug-in, and if you were to donate to a developer, this one really deserves it. His effort was extreme!

## ErsDrums (PC, VST)

Looking for completely synthesized drums that sound just like the vintage stuff that costs way too much on eBay? ErsDrums (www.bostreammail.net/ers/ersdrums.html; see Figure 5.9) does a wonderful job of emulating those videogame-sounding drums of old that make people shake their butts on the floor. And it's purely synthesized drums. As the website states, "No samples are used."

**Figure 5.9** If you love vintage drum machines, make sure you check out ErsDrums.

You get two kicks, two snares, two blipps (videogame sounds—awesome, eh?), one clap, one claves, one hi-hat, and one crash. What's also beautiful is that you can do separate outputs per drum, and you can even assign each drum its own MIDI channel!

Also, because ErsDrum is completely synthesized, you have the ability to continually make your own drums, your own patches, and so on. It's also perfect fodder for making your own loops, Rex files, and more.

Sadly, it's only available for the PC, but again, this is the perfect reason for Mac guys to get a Boot Camp partition or a virtual machine going. Imagine the sample possibilities!

## HTML Drum Machines

Bored at school, at work, or at your mother-in-law's house without any music software? Have an itch to create beats and no way to do it? Try checking out an online drum machine!

Drum machines are some of the many HTML5 and Flash-based instruments that have been appearing on the Internet over the past several years. Although the concept seems more like a lark, these drum machines are perfect opportunities for recording and sampling. Build up your own beat library absolutely for free.

Check out:

- Monkey Machine: www.rinki.net/pekka/monkey
- Unifix Cube Drum Machine: www.philtulga.com/unifix.html
- HTML5 Drum Kit: www.randomthink.net/labs/html5drums
- Sonic Charge, creators of the MicroTonic, Bitspeek, and Synplant, have the Patternarium, which plays real-time synthesized drum loops: soniccharge.com/patternarium

## Conclusion

From this wonderful selection of drum modules, you should have plenty of beat fodder to keep you going for a long time. Remember to keep an eye out for new stuff, though. You never know what may appear on the Net!

### Interview with Josh Pyle

**Could you give us a quick introduction with some of the albums, software packages, and singles you've been a part of?**

I'm Josh Pyle of Aphorism (*Surge*, 2009).

**How much experience have you had with free or open-source music plug-ins?**

I've had extensive experience with freeware plug-ins over the years, both for production on Aphorism tracks and for other projects, such as Audio Paradox. I've also used them for some sound-design projects.

**Is there a particular audio plug-in of which you are extremely fond? Feel free to list multiple ones.**

When used sparingly, glitch-based plug-ins and/or plug-ins that create generative beats can add an additional layer of complexity to a drum loop, a drone, a drum sequence, or even a synth or lead track. I really like a lot of the Smartelectronix freeware plug-ins, particularly SupaTrigga and Livecut.

I've also used the Green Oak Crystal synth on a number of tracks, which I've found to have unique abilities reminiscent of NI's ABSYNTH, while having very different sonic qualities and a very easy-to-use UI.

**Could you share a quick story about where this plug-in has really shined during your music creation/production work?**

When working on a track for the Tympanik *EO3* compilation, I was using a piano sample sent to me by friend and sometimes-collaborator Kris Rosentrater. Integrating the piano piece into a beat-driven track needed some additional glue to really capture the right aesthetic I was going for, fusing the piano with the programmed beats and loops. I wanted to add a looser element, so I layered different instances of SupaTrigga and Livecut on piano and loop channels in Ableton while emphasizing the synth lead lines.

**Is there a particular free/open-source virtual instrument of which you've become fond? Feel free to list multiple ones.**

Drool String Ukelele is an amazing, possibly legendary standalone app created by Shawn Hatfield (Twerk) for creating algorithmically generated pieces from samples and loops. This app is a lot of fun, giving you the ability to endlessly tweak numerous settings, including delays. I've come up with lots of ideas based on pieces created in Drool String. Using this app, I've created material that I eventually edited down, manipulated in Ableton, and incorporated into new Aphorism tracks. In fact, numerous tracks on *Surge* incorporate loops or beats that originated from sessions in Drool String.

**Have you had any difficulties installing or working with any of the free/open-source plug-ins that you've checked out?**

I never had any issues installing or working with them. The main plug-ins I've used have always functioned exactly as expected within the host application. Standalone apps have also worked exactly as expected. The interfaces were intuitive but not completely laid out—just enough to encourage curiosity and experimentation.

**Do you have any advice for beginner musicians/ producers working with free/open-source audio plug-ins?**

Always keep in mind the goal of creating original, interesting work. Push your limits, don't be afraid to experiment, and keep your focus on creating something new.

# 6 Niche Plug-Ins

There's a time for every kind of herb and spice when cooking. Sometimes you need thyme, sometimes basil, sometimes pepper. There are numerous spices and seasonings, and they all add a little something to the dish you are preparing. And really, the nutrients of the base food that you are preparing will be pretty much the same when it's all over with. I mean, chicken will still taste like chicken, beef will still taste like beef, and any other odd meat will still taste like chicken, because everything besides cow tastes like chicken anyway—right?

But the seasoning adds something, and it makes the people for whom you prepare your food react differently, too. We season to create some difference in the end—some fun, something besides plain old chicken or beef.

Music is no different than cooking in a lot of ways. You mix elements together and keep mixing until it sounds right. You keep adding things as you move along, and eventually you may get something that sounds just perfect!

Sometimes adding in odd and unpredictable elements can really add something to your creation. It can be that moment when you mistakenly added soy sauce instead of BBQ sauce, and suddenly you have an amazing-tasting dish that you never thought of.

In this chapter, I'd like to turn you on to just the kind of "spices" I'm referring to, in the form of music plug-ins. These plug-ins add that random element where you never really know what's going to happen—but it sounds either really great or like an immediate mess.

Because these are plug-ins, you can turn them off as soon as you decide they aren't the right ones, or you can rock them as much as you like on any song you want.

One thing that I've encountered is that many independent programmers tend to experiment far more than the major companies do. This makes sense, because a lot of the time software is being developed to follow market trends. Large companies have a staff, and they have to pay them, so they need money.

For individual programmers, this isn't a concern. They have fun working as they refine their craft. The end result benefits us all with these wild plug-ins/sounds/styles that no one thought of before.

Indeed, plug-ins are becoming responsible for a whole new wave of style. In much the same way that a Marshall stack changed guitar forever, plug-ins are doing so, too!

## Multi-FX Randomization Plug-Ins

I'd like to start off with a very specific form of FX plug-in that can add a random feel to your music, while still making it sound more than organic. This form of plug-in I will attempt to label as multi-FX, but really "randomization plug-ins" would probably be accurate as well. In fact, these plug-ins do both.

One minute your audio will sound as if it's going through a flange, the next second through a chorus, then through a delay. You never know what it will be, because you don't get to choose—the computer does!

There are also more than a few tricks for these types of plug-ins. You can, for example, run them in real time through your song or bounce the audio with the effect burned onto the audio so that you retain a snapshot of the randomization you like.

In the end, you'll probably come up with your own tricks anyway. I'll introduce you to some of these plug-ins, and as you learn about them, hopefully you'll join some of the many users who regard these plug-ins as the best kept secrets!

## DBGlitch (PC, VST)

Easily one of the most popular freeware plug-ins over the last decade is DBGlitch (illformed.org/plugins/glitch). In fact, it's so popular that it has inspired its own clothing line that I see people wearing from time to time in the more nerdy sections of the Bay Area.

What makes DBGlitch (see Figure 6.1) so interesting and worthwhile for your own plug-in collection is what it does for you. It takes any audio file and, in real time, runs it through a step sequencer that can rhythmically effect the audio file with any number of DJ effects at any moment.

**Figure 6.1** DBGlitch is an amazing plug-in that adds incredible randomization to your audio through a built-in step sequencer.

This is brilliant for sound designers because you can just let DBGlitch go for a while, render your song as an audio file, and then cut snippets of sounds. In the end, you get these really cool electro, organic, nightmarish sounds with which you can do anything.

What's also interesting is that you can choose the percentage of certain effects in terms of how likely they are to trigger. For example, you may want the flange to hit 75% of the time, whereas the bit crusher occurs only 50% of the time, and you never know when they will happen.

You might have noticed that there is no Mac or Linux version; however, the next application will fill this role for you Apple users.

## SupaTrigga (PC and Mac, VST/AU)

I've had many people ask me about a Mac version of DBGlitch, and sadly, it doesn't exist. But there are people who have made some plugins that come close to doing the same thing that DBGlitch does.

SupaTrigga (bram.smartelectronix.com/plugins.php?id=6) is one such free option. It doesn't have the intricate interface that DBGlitch has, but I think that may actually work better, in a sense. As you can see in Figure 6.2, the interface doesn't have a lot in terms of sliders and buttons, but the sound is very intricate. You just pop it in your session and let SupaTrigga take care of the rest.

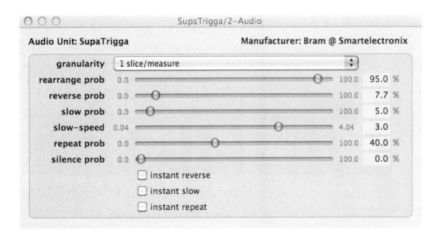

**Figure 6.2** SupaTrigga is not DBGlitch, but it is a close, free alternative if you are Mac only.

SupaTrigga rearranges audio files in real time with stuttering effects, reverse effects, and so on—all done to the tempo of your host sequencer. As with DBGlitch, you can tell SupaTrigga the percentage that you want certain effects to occur, if at all.

Adjusting the granularity as the song moves forward—or even during a live performance—can bring astounding effect and build to a song. For example, putting SupaTrigga on 128 slices per measure will essentially mangle your song; use this for a break and then switch back to 2 slices per measure to let things run normally. And what's great is that you can automate the granularity throughout your song!

### Thoughts on Multi-FX Randomization Plug-Ins

I find it comforting to know that some of the most influential plug-ins in underground electronic music were made underground, for the underground. And although these plug-ins may not initially seem like what you may be looking for, throwing something different or completely out of its element into something else can sometimes make the song—for example, throwing electric guitar into a classical piece. Normally it wouldn't work, but John Williams actually did it for a speeder chase in *Star Wars: Episode II*, and it helped achieve an edginess needed for that chase.

And besides, these plug-ins are completely free and take about a second to download (literally), so what will it hurt?

# MIDI-Controlled FX Plug-Ins

This type of plug-in is great because of the kind of control you get. You can tie FX to your MIDI controller and, with the touch of a key, drop nasty, game-changing effects into your mix, instrument, audio track—whatever you want, whenever you want.

For example, you drop one of these FX on an audio track and then you route a MIDI track to the audio track. When you play your MIDI keyboard, the effect on the audio track is triggered. It sounds complicated, but I'll explain more as I begin showing you these fine plug-ins.

## GetaBlitch Jr. (PC and Mac, VST)

In many forms of electronic music, gating, ducking, and so on have become quite prominent. The way gating works is that you rhythmically decrease the volume and increase the volume on an audio track. It's sort of like moving the volume up and down in rhythm on a stereo when a song is playing.

GetaBlitch Jr. (www.shuriken.se; see Figure 6.3) is a very simple plug-in that acts as a gate for audio, but with one small exception—you use a MIDI keyboard to open up the gate.

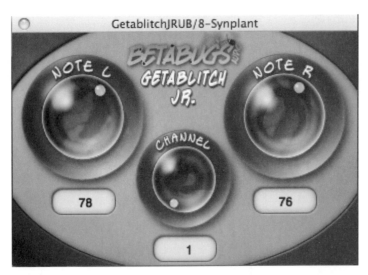

**Figure 6.3** GetaBlitch Jr. allows you to rhythmically enable and disable the audio signal coming into it in stereo.

Just so this makes sense, let me explain how a gate works. If an audio track is going through a gate, you will not be able to hear the audio track until you open the gate. What separates GetaBlitch Jr. is that you use your MIDI keyboard to open this gate. Press a specific key, and you can hear audio.

GetaBlitch Jr. goes even further, though, because there is a key assigned to the left audio signal of a channel and the right audio signal of a channel. This is perfect, because it allows you to gate in stereo. Press one key to hear the left and one key to hear the right. If you are playing the keyboard rhythmically, you can make some really interesting rhythmic texture.

For example, instantiate GetaBlitch Jr. on an instrument track that is playing sustained notes. On a separate MIDI track, trigger GetaBlitch Jr. to open and close. Every time you hit a key, you hear the sustained notes only as long as you hold down the key. Tapping the key over and over again, or rhythmically, will allow you to create patterns out of the sustained notes, almost as if the sustained audio is an entirely new part.

## SqakAttack (PC and Mac, VST)

Bear with me here—this one takes a little bit to wrap your head around. If this explanation doesn't help you, you can always check out the video at www.shuriken.se.

Like GetaBlitch Jr., SqakAttack (see Figure 6.4) is to be instantiated on an audio track as an FX plug-in. And like GetaBlitch Jr., SqakAttack needs a MIDI track routed to control the audio FX plug-in with a controller.

**Figure 6.4** SqakAttack allows you to play an audio buffer to get some crazy electronic stuttering effects on your audio track.

What occurs next is truly fascinating. When you start playing keys on your MIDI keyboard controller, musically you are "glitching" the audio. For example, if you press the lowest key on the keyboard, you can hear SqakAttack slowly stuttering the audio. As you move up the octaves, the stutter gets faster until it becomes musical.

I've used this all over the place—for example, when distorting and holding back certain parts of drum loops in real time, when creating quick glitchy effects in vocals, and when creating new melodies out of other melodies.

I also recommend combining SqakAttack with other effects while you use it. Use it with some delay, distortion, and bit crushers. Because it is such a unique effect, combinations with other effects definitely will make something new and even more unique.

Of equal interest is the fact that the only other developer I have seen come close to creating an effect like this is Access Music, with their Virus TI line. One effect that came after Virus TI's release, with an update, was the Atomizer effect, which does something very similar to SqakAttack.

Virus TI will cost you a few thousand dollars, whereas SqakAttack will cost you a few seconds of your time. Nice, eh?

## StormGate (PC and Mac, VST/AU)

StormGate's power lies in its envelope-style step sequencer. You simply draw curves into the step sequencer's pattern and press Play. Instantly, you will hear audio (preferably sustained) played back in the form of a rhythmic pattern. The curve moving up means that the volume is high and audio is being allowed through. When the curve or line is low in the pattern area, that means little to no audio is allowed through.

What's even better about StormGate (www.araldfx.com; see Figure 6.5) is the fact that you can chain together multiple patterns that you've created, or even use one of the many banks that come with the plug-in already.

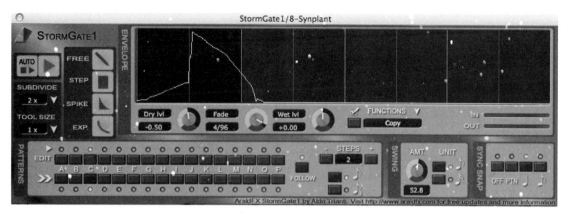

**Figure 6.5** StormGate turns any audio into a rhythmic pattern with its amazing step sequencer.

For the most part, StormGate is a one-trick pony, but don't think of gating as something that you have to use only for electronic music. Throwing in some rhythmic gates on beats, vocals, and so on can be just the right effect for a break or other parts of the song that you want to step out.

Although StormGate is not MIDI controlled, it does follow very closely what the other two plug-ins mentioned in this section do, so I thought it appropriate to mention these together.

# FX Classified as "Other"

Some plug-ins make things sound pretty, some plug-ins enhance a sound, and some plug-ins just completely rip up a sound completely. The plug-ins in this section do just that: They make things sound much noisier and dirtier, and in some cases, they completely change the sound.

Why would you want distorted, dirty, ripped-apart sounds? Well, there may be times when you want an edge or a contrast to your music. And there may be other times when the vocals, the drums, or a synth need that extra push to make them stand out.

There may also be times when you just want some sound FX, and you need them quickly. These plug-ins really help in just such a situation!

Let's take a quick walk through the dirtier plug-ins of the bunch.

## KTGranulator (PC and Mac, VST/AU)

Granular synthesizers break down chunks of audio into small portions (each about a millisecond long). These portions are known as *grains*. Where it gets interesting is when you decide to play back a single grain, which will essentially cause a rapid loop of one millisecond, or you want to play a couple of loops. What results is a very smooth, almost otherworldly audio image of small and large portions of audio. But it gets even more interesting when you start playing with pitch and so on.

KTGranulator (koen.smartelectronix.com/KTGranulator; see Figure 6.6) essentially samples audio in real time and plays it back in real time with

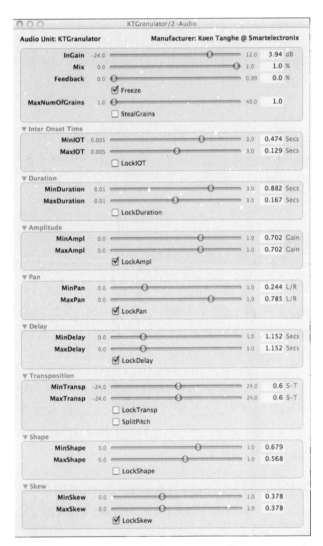

**Figure 6.6** KTGranulator is a free granular effects processor that allows you to seriously mangle your audio.

granular processing. Because it's in real time, you can manipulate audio as it plays, speeding up playback, slowing it down, or using quick bursts or sustained noise. In the end, what comes out of KTGranulator ends up being completely different from what you originally put in.

One way I like to use KTGranulator is to automate its freeze function for the certain portions of my songs. On vocals, it grabs a small grain of audio—or several, depending on my settings—and I can just start mangling it during a break or buildup. It sounds otherworldly, and it's a lot of fun.

It's also cool to know that you can use KTGranulator as a delay or echo. This can be a wonderful effect for vocals, but also for drumbeats. Because you can have KTGranulator play back its echoes in different pitches, you can create some wonderful textures out of raw audio.

## Berrtill (PC and Mac, VST)

Remember those old Speak & Spell toys? They were usually grimy with children's handprints, sitting in a toy box, half broken, but occasionally pulled out and enjoyed for a minute?

Those devices, shown in Figure 6.7, were in some cases continually loved by children all the way up until adulthood. These adults, who became musicians, found new ways to employ, modify, and abuse the little red-and-yellow portable electronic.

When I say *abuse*, I mean that people began modifying their Speak & Spells to give them more of an edge, to add new "music-friendly" features to them. Essentially, they converted a children's game into speaking monstrosity—and this sound caught on.

Berrtill (www.shuriken.se; see Figure 6.8) is a distortion plug-in that seeks to emulate a modified, or "circuit-bent," Speak & Spell or other such device—believe me, the Speak & Spell is not the only one.

With its skull-adorned knobs and simple layout, it looks just about like it sounds—nasty. Knob adjustments such as Clip and Drive are fairly well known as amplifier settings, but from there on, it's doing

**Figure 6.7** Speak & Spell, a loved toy of an older generation, was later used and abused in the name of music.

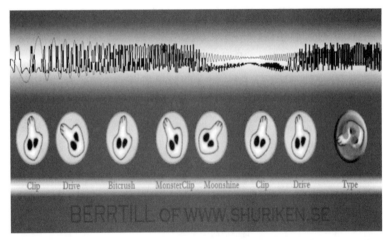

**Figure 6.8** Berrtill seeks to emulate the distorted 8-bit persona of the circuit-bent Speak & Spell and other such devices.

something else entirely. The Bitcrush knob erodes your audio signal from a lovely 44.1-kHz (or even higher) sample rate to something akin to a Nintendo Game Boy that has been beaten several times but somehow still works.

Basically, Berrtill makes everything sound as if it came from the speaker of a damaged Speak & Spell. It sounds terrible beyond belief, but to some of us, it's a beautiful thing.

This effect is great for leads, vocals, drum loops, and individual hits. Just don't apply it to something that you want to retain a low or high end, such as a hi-hat or kick, because it does make things pretty midrange.

## Conclusion

It has been my goal to expose you to some of the FX plug-ins that are really off the beaten path. In my opinion, they are true gems. They may be a little difficult to understand at first, but once you wrap your head around them, you'll wonder how you lived without them. They also add to your sound; they give you something unique.

As you learn to find your own plug-ins through the resources listed in the next chapter, keep an eye out for more esoteric and outside-the-box plug-ins as you move forward. What I've introduced you to isn't even close to being all of them. There are thousands out there, but these are some that I really like and hope you enjoy!

**Interview with Orren Merton**

**Could you give us a quick introduction with some of the albums, software packages, and singles you've been a part of?**

I'm Orren Merton, singer/guitarist/songwriter in a few mean and moody rock bands.

My first band, the gothic-rock Darkling Thrush, released two EPs (*Myriad* and *Segue*). My current band, a more industrial-rock band, Ember After, has released an album (*Grasping At Straws*), and a new EP is nearly out the door (to be titled *The Shallow EP*).

I've also done the soundtrack for an *extremely* indie, low-budget movie named *Return to Innocence*.

As far as audio software goes, I've done beta-testing and tech writing for quite a few audio software companies and a couple of hardware companies, and I may have done some presets in there for them as well, but those change all the time, so I'm not sure.

**How much experience have you had with free or open-source music plug-ins?**

One of the very first plug-in synthesizers that I ever used—and this must be more than a decade ago—was the beautiful and brilliant Crystal, a free synth that is still updated regularly, even though the developer is now lead programmer for a major for-profit audio software house. It was not only fantastic, but it pushed my limits creatively and also helped teach me about synthesis. I can't say enough good things about Crystal!

In the audio processor category, I have and still use nearly every plug-in from Destroy FX, all free.

**Is there a particular audio plug-in of which you are extremely fond? Feel free to list multiple ones.**

See above. Some of the Destroy FX stuff, such as Buffer Override, is a bit long in the tooth now that there are so many stuttering-style plug-ins, but it's still a quick, down-and-dirty, great way to get a quick, wild stutter-edit sound!

**Could you share a quick story about where this plug-in has really shined during your music creation/production work?**

For the song "Only You Remain," it was sounding a bit too much like a standard ballad, but a little Buffer Override on the loops, and it sounded like something very modern. Not the sort of plug-in you need often, but that's exactly why it's great that there's a free plug-in that works—buying a $400 plug-in you'll use on a couple songs isn't very cost-effective.

**Is there a particular free/open-source virtual instrument of which you've become fond? Feel free to list multiple ones.**

Crystal is good enough to give any commercial synth a run for its money!

**Could you share a quick story about where this instrument has really shined during your music creation/production work?**

A lot of commercial plug-ins, in order to make sure that potential buyers like what they hear, have user interfaces that guide you into making only "pleasant" sounds. Since Crystal isn't really competing with them, it dispenses with that sort of UI "babysitting," which means that it's very easy to move just a few sliders and get a completely odd or new sound that you've never heard before. More than one time working on *Grasping At Straws*, I liked what I was writing, but it was sounding a bit too "routine," if that makes sense. Put on Crystal, pull up a sound close to what I want, and without much effort at all, I'd have something very fresh-sounding!

**Have you had any difficulties installing or working with any of the free/open-source plug-ins that you've checked out?**

No—most have installers just like any commercial plug-in or can simply be dragged into the correct plug-ins folder manually. In fact, one of the biggest problems with many commercial plug-ins is issues caused by their dongles or authorization schemes, so free and open-source stuff tends to be easier to work with, not more difficult.

**Do you have any advice for beginner musicians/ producers working with free/open-source audio plug-ins?**

Don't let the price tag fool you—let your ears be the judge. Crystal, for example, is a labor of love from a guy whose work for a major company costs big bucks. To dismiss it for not costing a lot is a huge mistake. Especially if you're collaborating with other musicians, free plug-ins are a great way to make sure that everyone working together has the same processors and instruments in their DAW.

# 7 Where to Find More

We've covered a lot of really cool plug-ins that I hope will change your music-making process for the better. I hope the new DAW that cost you little to nothing is redefining your workflow. I hope the free synths are adding new color and magic to your sound. I also hope that you are making great beats with drum machines, using your samples and so much more.

I have introduced one addiction into your life, though—free/inexpensive software. And now that you've had a taste of it, you'll undoubtedly want more. This chapter contains resources that will showcase, guide you to, and even review free plug-ins as they are released. These are websites, magazines, and online resources I've used for years, and they have brought me endless fun. And now, I'm giving them to you.

I would like to stress one thing, though. Don't get so wrapped up in the accumulation of gear, plug-ins, and software that you forget the entire reason why you got into all of this—music.

Once we get a taste of something, we want more, more, more! We pick up the new toy, use it for a minute, and throw it back in the toy box. Remember, though, that each little toy you find—either on the Internet, in a magazine, or wherever—was lovingly created by someone who spent a lot of time on each piece of software.

Regardless of how much it cost you, push the software and try to discover an alternate purpose for it. You spent the time to find it, so now spend the time to know it. There are always hidden uses, features, and more that could change your way of working. There are tons of settings, and you may find one that defines your sound!

I advise you spend at least a week (if not more) with a new plug-in within your song-making regimen. If it crashes your system... well, then I wouldn't spend too much time on it. But if it works flawlessly, push it! If it's a synth, try using it for more than one part in your song. Is it better for bass parts or lead parts?

If you're trying out an FX plug-in, does it sound better on guitar, vocals, synths, or drums? Does it add to it or take away from it?

When you're working with a new host application, such as a DAW, does it help you write a song more quickly or mix more quickly? Does it sound better? Does it have a feature you've always wanted that your current application doesn't have? Maybe you could use this application for mixing and your other one for writing? Maybe you could have this app on one machine and your regular app on another?

These are all questions and concepts to which I hope you'll give some thought as you move forward. Now, let me show you how to fish!

## The Websites

If anything has contributed to the proliferation of music software, it's music websites. After all, most of us want to read the experts' opinions on something before we waste our valuable time, right?

At first, these sites were just fan sites run by people like you and me who have a passion for music software. As time moved on, certain sites became the "go-to" places for specific types of information. In this section, I'll show you my "go-to" places.

## KVR Audio

What started out as a simple fan-made resource became a major hub for music software information. KVR Audio (kvraudio.com; see Figure 7.1) has been around for a long, long time.

**Figure 7.1** KVR Audio not only provides a wealth of information on music plug-ins of all sorts, it also is a full-fledged database.

KVR Audio began as a web-design project, amusingly enough, by the brains behind the project, Ben Turl. Originally, Ben just wanted a place to showcase and contribute some patches he'd made for the original VST plug-ins, such as Steinberg's Neon, LM-4, and such.

Through website feedback and movement, Ben soon realized that many more people were interested in sharing their patches, plug-ins, and software. He started reporting from his site on new plug-ins, sound collections, and so on.

As the number of VST plug-ins increased dramatically and KVR began to include additional types of plug-ins, such as Audio Units, DirectX, and so on, Ben added a plug-ins database to handle all of the instruments, FX, and so on that were popping up.

Eventually, KVR Audio was purchased by Muse Research, a well-known company responsible for the Receptor, Receptor 2, and so on. Because the Receptor 2 is a tour-friendly, rack-based VST host for guitarists and whoever else wants to plug their instrument into it, this was a match made in heaven.

Ben still runs KVR Audio for Muse Research, and he still gives it the same love and attention it truly deserves.

Now, let's talk about why you should pay a lot of attention to this website.

### *The Database*

The database alone is a wonderful reason to go to this website frequently. Just by experimenting with different search criteria, you can find thousands of plug-ins, applications, and more (see Figure 7.2).

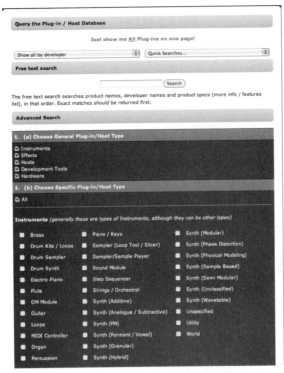

**Figure 7.2** The mighty KVR database. Use it to find any plug-in that you ever knew—or didn't know—existed.

The database includes software for free, software for purchase, and links to demos. There are even user reviews of plug-ins.

As you experiment with searching through the database, make sure to check off the kind of software you are looking for. Will it be drums? Synthesizer? Will it be free, for purchase, or all the above?

The database is full-fledged and very comprehensive. It has served me and many others users well. Now that you know about it, you should use it, too!

### The Forums

The KVR user forums are highly moderated, and I mean this in the best possible way. Users are encouraged to be friendly and helpful in guiding other users to answers they seek regarding plug-ins and music creation.

I cannot stress enough the importance of being part of an online community when you're learning something new—or even if you're a seasoned professional. We all go through moments when we really need the answer to a problem, and who better to ask than other people just like us who are doing the same thing at the same moment?

There are also tons of developers who hang out in the KVR forums. This is a great place to find out firsthand what is new, what new updates are coming, and so on.

Finally, the forums are a great way not only to make friends, but also to share your music! What a novel thought, eh? Pop up a link to a new song you just finished and get some feedback. Who knows? The link might be passed on to someone who could really do something for you and that new song!

## Create Digital Music

Whereas KVR Audio tends to post more or less general release information, Create Digital Music (createdigitalmusic.com; see Figure 7.3) comes in and not only reports release information, but also fills you in on everything else.

**Figure 7.3** Create Digital Music is an amazing resource for what's new, cool, and unique.

Peter Kirn is the author of *Real World Digital Audio* (Peachpit Press, 2005) and writes for *Macworld, Keyboard,* and *Computer Music* magazines. He's also an inspiring musician who started Create Digital Music. Since the beginning, he has covered literally every facet of electronic music that you can imagine. From making music on Game Boys to new announcements from major software developers, Create Digital Music has its hands in everything.

I love this website. They really do report on everything that comes out of a speaker. They also take it further, with interviews and an amazing relationship with their readers. The photographs are always well done, and the overall design has a simple but lovely aesthetic.

Beyond publishing great articles, though, they are unbiased in their reviews. And because they are fans and creators, just like us, they voice their opinions in the articles, which tend to resonate with other creators as well.

Because Create Digital Music is technically a blog, you can post your opinion at the end of each article and see what everyone else is saying as well. Additionally, they have a forum of articulate, creative, and highly knowledgeable individuals.

However, to get back to why this is a great resource for software, Create Digital Music regularly spotlights shareware, freeware, and up-and-coming software. This often happens well before everyone else has jumped on it.

If you want to learn and be up on what's current, you definitely check out Create Digital Music.

### iusethis

Where KVR Audio is a compendium of everything plug-in and music related, iusethis (iusethis.com; see Figure 7.4) is a database of everything operating system related.

**Figure 7.4** iusethis.com is a large database of applications for PC and Mac—and more!

If you go to iusethis on a PC, you will arrive at a website/database with software for the PC. If you go there on Mac, it's all Mac-based software.

In addition to music software, the site features every kind of software, with a keen rating system that helps you decide whether to check out a piece of software.

One thing to note is that iusethis has every kind of software on it—software for purchase, software for free, trials, demos, and so on. However, they do mark what is freeware, shareware, and so on.

I have gone to this website periodically for years, when I'm looking for something new or when I'm looking for an app that will achieve a specific purpose. For example, when I was looking for an alternative to Microsoft Word, I went to iusethis and looked up "word processing" to see what applications appeared.

I have found plenty of music software as well. Some of it isn't as specialized, but when you're a freelance sound designer/writer, you look for anything unique, right?

Regardless of what you are looking for, I highly suggest bookmarking this page. You never know when you'll need to find a specific app for a specific purpose, or you may find some cool music app no one has discovered yet.

## Magazines

Although some might consider printed magazines a thing of the past—and believe me when I tell you that I am becoming one of them—there are still some magazines that I'd like to list here. I think they are valid purchases due to their content and insight.

Honestly, I think that people get confused about music columnists and authors (like me). I think they get the idea that because we're writing a book or an article on a piece of software or hardware, we just read through the manual and disregard our past experience.

This is far from true, and all of the magazines I'm listing in this section are filled with material from pro musicians who have a lot to share and who want to see the music industry grow with competence and originality.

In addition to this desire for growth, all of the musicians writing for these magazines love toys just as much as the rest of us do, and they want to get the word out on new software. Believe me, there's a lot of free software mentioned in these magazines—as well as demos, upgrades, and more!

## Computer Music

One of the friendliest music magazines out there also tends to be one of the most generous. *Computer Music* magazine (see Figure 7.5) is beautifully compiled with tutorials that are lovingly made. And here's the clincher: The software that they use for these tutorials is, in most cases, included on a DVD with the actual magazine! That's right—*Computer Music* magazine ships with a DVD full of

**Figure 7.5** *Computer Music* magazine is not only chock-full of great tips, tutorials, and reviews, it also has a DVD full of apps, plug-ins, and sounds.

sounds, applications, and plug-ins. Although that alone should entice you to buy it, let me move back to the tutorials, because the tutorials rock!

You can learn from guys who give you step-by-step walkthroughs on how to achieve a sound from a certain artist and who tell you how to perform new techniques with mainstream apps and those they include for free.

All this sounds great, but there's one more reason to seriously consider this magazine. You may know that music magazines often get to try all the new software and hardware first. Given that the writers are all musicians, wouldn't it be nice to get their take on the hardware and software they see and use—even before it's on the market?

## Electronic Musician

I have been a fan of *Electronic Musician* (see Figure 7.6) for years. They feature in-depth interviews, reviews, and tutorials. And although they may not ship the magazine with a DVD included, as *Computer Music* does, their website has a section you should not ignore.

**Figure 7.6** *Electronic Musician* is one of the oldest magazines covering keyboards and computers.

You can visit the Downloads of the Month section to guide you to new and exciting products. And although these downloads are usually demos or dumbed-down versions of the actual plug-in or application, *Electronic Musician* does tend to have some special coupon codes if you read the fine print closely.

## Other Resources

There are some more obvious resources for finding new and cool plug-ins. In this section, let me point out some of them for you. You never know what might be right under your nose.

### Google

Google brings anything you are looking for to your fingertips instantly. Because this is the case, why not use it to find new software, plug-ins, and applications?

However, when you're looking around, make sure you're smart. Don't download something from some site saying "Cubase 5.0 for free." Odds are, if it sounds too good to be true, it is. And even if it *is* free, you are most likely downloading some skanky beta with questionable reliability that is riddled with viruses.

You're better off saving your money, because if your computer is infected by viruses, the money that you spend on the repair likely would've adequately covered whatever you were trying to download for free instead of paying for it.

Aside from my reprisal of rants about pirated software, there are tons of sites out there that host really good free VST plug-ins, AU plug-ins, and more. Try doing a search sometime: Enter "Free VST Plug-ins" or "Free AU Plug-ins" (see Figure 7.7). See what comes up!

**Figure 7.7** Google puts anything you want at your fingertips. Why not look for more?

When you find one you like, go over to KVR Audio and search for the plug-in in the database. If it's legit and seems worth your time, grab it and try it out!

## Friends and Other Musicians

One thing I've learned in this industry is to never be afraid to network. And after you've made a competent new friend, ask what he uses. I've found some killer plug-ins just by keeping in contact with musician friends. They point out good stuff to me; I point out good stuff to them. Share a little info, and you'll be surprised by what you get back!

## Paid Software on Which You Can Expand

Actually buying software can also pay off in ways that you may never have thought of. Companies such as Propellerhead are known for offering deals, freebies, and more to registered users of their programs (Reason, Record, and so on). They also host a dedicated list of ReFills, which are sound packs, instrument patches, templates, and so on for use in Reason, shown in Figure 7.8.

**Figure 7.8** Reason has tons of ReFills available for free.

Image-Line, the company responsible for FL Studio, shown in Figure 7.9, also has tons of plug-ins you can access just by purchasing FL Studio (with its lifetime free upgrades).

**Figure 7.9**   Tons of plug-ins come with FL Studio, as well as demos and more.

Ableton Live, shown in Figure 7.10, has a special version of Max/MSP that allows you to create your own and refine Ableton Live instruments and FX. (It's next on my list of purchases.) This is handy because you can also download and install instruments, FX processors, MIDI FX, and more that have been made by other users. This is an application that will keep on giving for years.

Similarly, Native Instruments' Reaktor, shown in Figure 7.11, has huge numbers of instruments and FX that have been building up for years. By simply owning Reaktor, you have access to an amazingly large library of simulated hardware that will keep you busy and keep your appetite for free gear.

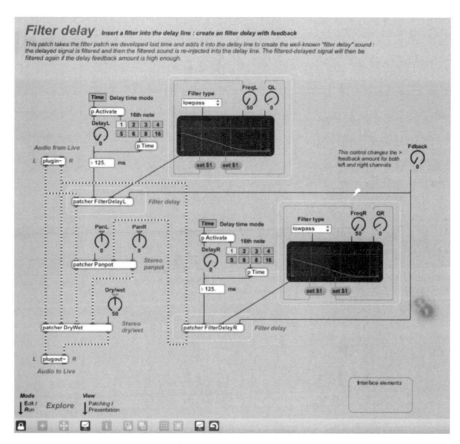

**Figure 7.10** Max/MSP for Ableton Live lets you build and install other instruments, FX, and so on that other users have made.

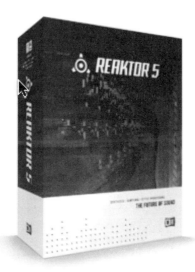

**Figure 7.11** Native Instruments' Reaktor lets you create instruments and FX and gives you access to a vast library of instruments and FX made by other users.

## Conclusion

Hopefully, you've gained some insight into what is out there for free, where to look, and what you're looking for. In this book, I tried to show you some great plug-ins and apps, but remember, technology is rapidly moving forward. There's a new announcement every day, and it would behoove you to keep an eye on some of the websites I've listed.

**Interview with Peter Kirn**

**Could you give us a quick introduction with some of the albums, software packages, and singles you've been a part of?**

My name is Peter Kirn. I run createdigitalmusic.com and createdigitalmotion.com—online magazine/communities for people making music and visuals with technolog— and the noisepages.com community platform. (In fact, all of this runs on free software—Red Hat Enterprise Linux, nginx, PHP, MySQL, and WordPress.)

I'm also a contributing editor to *Keyboard* and have contributed to *Macworld*, *Make*, *Popular Science*, *Wax Poetics*, and *Computer Music*.

I teach music and visual creation, currently at Parsons The New School for Design as well as at workshops around the world. I'm a classically trained composer, finishing a PhD in composition at the City University of New York Graduate Center.

I've done a lot of music for dance, working with choreographers such as Bessie-winner Christopher Williams. Depending on when this comes out, my solo electronic album *End of Train Device* should be out. And I still write for instruments and voices when I can, not just electronics.

I've also been a contributor to free software, most recently involved in libpd, the embeddable Pure Data that works everywhere from Android to Processing.

**How much experience have you had with free or open-source music plug-ins?**

I'm actually a relatively recent convert to free software plug-ins, now that I'm finally really happy with working on Linux. Two hosts have really changed working with free plug-ins on Linux: Ardour and its superb hybrid free-proprietary variation Harrison Mixbus, and now Renoise.

**Is there a particular audio plug-in of which you are extremely fond? Feel free to list multiple ones.**

I'm indebted to Dave Phillips (*Linux Journal*) for turning me on to Tom Szilagyi's incredible IR convolution reverb. It's a no-nonsense convolution plug-in loaded with useful impulses, and—increasingly essential to me—it supports the new, savvy LV2 format. I believe LV2 is the best bet for free plug-in development going forward.

I'm also a big fan of the Calf plug-ins.

Ardour creator Paul Davis pointed me to Barry's Satan Maximizer. You definitely don't want this beast on the main bus, but if you want to add crunchy distortion to percussion, it's brilliant.

I strongly recommend heading to the plug-ins recommended for Ardour for the best reference. There are countless good, simple, bread-and-butter plug-ins, and one will invariably wind up being invaluable on some project. Kudos to Ardour, too, for grouping these by category and developer when you run the host. It's the best way to look for plugs. (See ardour.org/plugins.)

It's especially nice to grab the LV2 plugs—I'd start there, since the whole collection could be overwhelming.

Also, although they're proprietary, I think linuxDSP deserves some recognition. They bring really serious, polished plug-ins to the Linux OS, and I found them essential to finishing my most recent album.

Although they're not open source, linuxDSP could make the difference between comfortably using Linux for production and not. They've also been good citizens, contributing back to the projects on which they work. Harrison Mixbus is also worth calling out: It's a perfect example of the potential of synergy between a free software product (Ardour) and proprietary code. It's the only time I've ever seen a developer completely replace the mixing console in a DAW. What you get is an extraordinary deal ($70), thanks in no small part to

Ardour's open business model, and you get the mixing-desk workflow not only missing in Ardour but in other DAWs, generally, and some terrific effects. And in turn, it makes using free software much more viable—you can still make use of all these other free plug-ins, without feeling as if you'll have to fall back on your Mac or Windows system to finish the track to your satisfaction.

But the single most important tool to me remains Pd. The funny thing about working with free software, working with open-ended software, is that you get an opportunity to build exactly what you need rather than try to whittle down a bunch of monolithic tools to what you need.

Combined with JACK, Pd is a powerful way to build your own synths, effects, sequencers, and the like. It's increasingly my go-to tool.

**Could you share a quick story about where this plug-in has really shined during your music creation/production work?**

I'll turn back to Pd. I found that I was frustrated using proprietary software in performance. I still love tools such as Ableton Live, but because these are such big tools, I found that I was struggling with them a bit in live use. You couldn't absolutely guarantee stability because of the number of variables, and very often, I found I couldn't get the feeling that I was really using an instrument.

Pd has absolutely changed that for me. I can build, from scratch, something really simple, so that I focus on a few basic parameters and concentrate on controlling those live. I'm even more excited now that we can embed Pd in other contexts—so you can build a UI with Processing, or load an entire Pd patch on, say, an Android tablet.

Rjlib, the GPL-licensed collection of patches from RjDj for Pd, is especially nice. The truth is, you're not going to invent a reverb or invent a two-oscillator synth every single time you launch Pd. If you do try that, you probably won't ever get anything done, and it's not as though you'll find some new way of doing these things. I like to get to making some sounds and then try to do something original or innovative—and very often it has to do with finding an interesting sample or compositional idea. So, Rjlib can be really revolutionary.

You find a module that just does a simple delay and then build your own strange sequencer around it. It's incredible as a productivity booster.

I love the power of these big tools in a studio. But what I find is, when you go live, you want less, not more. If you build just the basics of what you need to play, you can really make the computer about your gesture and your input. Computer music performance feels again like playing a musical instrument—or at least a compositional instrument—and less like flying a jumbo jet on autopilot.

**Is there a particular free/open-source virtual instrument that you've become fond of? Feel free to list multiple ones.**

I think that's covered above—Pd.

**Have you had any difficulties installing or working with any of the free/open-source plug-ins that you've checked out?**

I really like working with a Linux distro that does the work for you. For me, that means either Fedora with Planet CCRMA or Ubuntu. I actually don't like the audio-specific distros as much because I find they have too much installed by default, but those can be useful for beginners. Honestly, it's worth trying live discs and so on, just to find what you like.

**Do you have any advice for beginner musicians/ producers working with free/open-source audio plug-ins?**

The best advice for beginners is, start with JACK. Use JACK as your audio engine, and you'll find you resolve a lot of problems. Read the documentation: You need to do a couple of tweaks to give JACK real-time audio priority, even on the vanilla Linux kernel. And I don't advise people to muck around with the real-time kernel anymore, either. The vanilla kernel now delivers stable audio performance, and it's a lot friendlier than the real-time kernel to configure.

Use JACK, use Ardour, focus on a few LV2 plug-ins, try Mixbus or linuxDSP or Renoise even though they're proprietary, see how much you can build in Pd, and I think you'll be really musically productive in Linux and free software.

**Any speculation on where you see open-source audio applications and plug-ins going in the future?**

I think Ardour is about to get a whole lot bigger with Ardour 3 and MIDI. And I think Mixbus will continue to give it a huge boost among people who were otherwise afraid of free software.

I'm hopeful that we'll see a UI overhaul in Pd. Already, the work Hans-Christoph Steiner has done with the existing UI and plug-ins makes it way more usable. Updates are coming fast and furious, and the whole tool is better. And I think libpd could broaden Pd's appeal, too, alongside other tools such as Csound and SuperCollider. You can really invent new audiovisual instruments now with these tools, even as a fairly modest programmer. And that, to me, is the great appeal of using a computer.

**Is there anything you're hoping you will see from the open-source community? A pie-in-the-sky plug-in that would make life complete?**

Not really. I'd rather make it easier to build what you need with Pd than find the one thing that fits everyone—it's clear that doesn't exist. And although all the current distros are promising, we need broader support for at least one distro to make it friendlier for people to use as a vanilla Linux music install.

# Appendix A: More Must-Haves

Once your computer situation is squared away, you've decided on what DAW to start with, and you have an audio interface that suits your needs, it's time to consider the rest of the peripheral hardware that is essential to any music-production studio. All the items discussed in this appendix make up the backbone of your studio. But just like your computer and interface, they will be either replaced or upgraded as you and your studio grow. Regardless, it's always smart to investigate what's out there so you can make solid, *informed* decisions when making your first purchases in each category. After reading through each item, I urge you to hit the Net to explore what's out there; also, be sure to ask fellow studio mavens for recommendations. As you hunt for and gather information, definitely consider the positives and negatives, but in the end don't be afraid to go against the grain. Making great music is all about breaking the rules!

## Other Essential Studio Hardware

In addition to what we covered in the book proper, there are several other pieces of gear that will help you enhance your studio. This section takes a look at other essential hardware, including studio monitors, headphones, microphones, and MIDI controllers. We discussed MIDI controllers briefly in Chapter 1, but this appendix will cover them in more detail.

### Studio Monitors

Your audio interface will ensure that sounds going into and coming out of your computer will be delivered with professional results. To hear what's traveling to and fro at optimum levels, you'll need at least one pair of professional-grade near-field monitors (see Figure A.1). At the top of the list of reasons why monitors of this level (also referred to as *reference* or *studio* monitors) are required is the fact these enclosures will deliver your work with a flat response—meaning that these monitors will not in any way color your production by reproducing a distorted (negatively altered)

**Figure A.1**  If you think the speakers that came with your computer will accurately reflect your studio efforts, think again. A pair of studio-grade near-field monitors is what you need, such as this set of Studiophile BX8a Deluxe monitors from M-Audio.

version of your work or by adding or subtracting any frequencies in an attempt to enhance it. Instead, you'll get an accurate reproduction of your production with minimal distortion (not the cool-guy guitar-player kind, just the absence of inaccurate changes to frequency content or amplitude levels). When shopping for a pair (or two) of monitors, bring along something you can plug into them that you're acutely familiar with in terms of the frequency content. For instance, pack your iPod loaded with an MP3 that you can use as reference. Just make sure the iPod's EQ setting is set flat and that you have the correct cabling to plug a single ⅛-inch stereo out to a pair of mono ¼-inch ins. This may require a Y cable and an ⅛-inch–¼-inch adapter, which can be easily found at your local Radio Shack (now called The Shack) or may even be on hand at the store that carries the monitors.

Other notable features found in studio-grade monitors include the following:

- Multiple built-in power amps dedicated to the high and low frequencies, making up what's called a tuned system. This is facilitated by a component called an *active crossover*, which divides the incoming signal into these two parts and then routes them to their appropriate drivers—woofers for the lows and tweeters for the highs.

- They usually come in compact enclosures, making it possible to integrate them into studio spaces that don't have much of just that.

- Shielding of some sort to prevent noise most likely related to your computer monitor.

- A robust design that allows for the consistent, stable reproduction of your inconsistent, un-mastered tracks, which will be inherently riddled with sudden volume bursts and sporadic moments of intense frequency explosions.

When sussing out power requirements in your studio, be sure to include some extra plugs in your plans for your monitors. More than likely, the monitors you choose will be active, which means they contain one or more components inside their enclosure that require AC power. The aforementioned tuned system—also known as a bi-amplified system—is active as it contains an array of power amps that need, well, power. All these attributes combined are what ensure a clean, accurate reproduction of the overall sound.

**Who's Driving This Thing, Anyway?**    Before exiting the realm of studio monitors, and in keeping with our "informed decision" mantra, it's important to consider a key component: the *driver*. As you read through the specifications while shopping for your first pair of monitors, you'll find that knowledge of this component will serve you well.

The driver is the spherical apparatus staring you in the face from inside the monitor enclosure. The various components that make up a driver are on display in Figure A.2, which will serve as a much-needed visual aid as you read through this brief explanation.

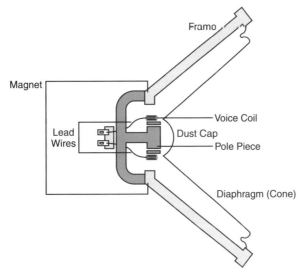

**Figure A.2**  The spherical apparatus called the driver eyeballing you at every turn is actually doing the bulk of the work within your studio monitor. To discover how the driver does what it does, consult this cross-section as you read on.

What you have is a lightweight, cylindrical *voice coil* comprised of fine copper wire that's mounted as such and can move freely within a magnetic field. The magnetic field is provided by the substantial permanent *magnet* at the base of the driver, which has a *pole piece* protruding from the center that is surrounded by voice coil. The *speaker cone* or *diaphragm* is attached to the voice coil and also to the *outer frame* or *basket* and has a dark center circle called the *dust cap*. To get this whole thing working, an electrical current is sent to the voice coil via the *lead wires,* making it electromagnetic. Once this happens, the voice coil and the magnet interact with each other through mechanical force, causing the coil to move back and forth, thus moving the connected diaphragm. The movement of this diaphragm creates the sound waves that travel through the air and deliver audio information to our ears. This is how sound is reproduced once it has been converted back to analog by the DAC in your audio interface and sent out the main outs via speaker cables.

**Headphones**

It's a safe bet that you already have a pair (or more) of headphones in your possession. Be it the earbuds (yes, those are headphones) that came with your iPod or that ubiquitous black set that seems to pop up at every turn, another safe bet is you probably haven't put much thought (or money) into them. As you may have already guessed, that needs to change. It's imperative that your studio have at least one pair of studio-grade headphones, and here are some reasons why:

- Starting with the obvious: They're a portable, discreet listening device. Whether you're using them as a part of your mobile studio or to work on your tracks in another studio, they give you the peace of mind that you're equipped with a listening device you're familiar with. Headphones easily go where you go, and their for-your-ears-only design is handy for those many times you'll need to isolate your work in progress from your co-inhabitants or neighbors who actually sleep at night while you're mixing your next opus.

- Speaking of isolation it's standard protocol to whip out a pair of headphones when recording overdubs (secondary tracks) if you have no other way to isolate miked sources.

- You may be listening to a mix and think you hear something that isn't right, something deep within the mix that's too tough to identify while listening to your near-fields. Fear not: A pair of closed-back (explained in a moment) headphones will help shine an audible floodlight on whatever anomaly is lurking in the sonic shadows.

- Many music lovers, including you, listen to music with some sort of speaker system attached to their heads—probably more so than ever before, considering all the digital toys we have to play with. So, if you're planning to bring your music to the people—especially people who use headphones often—it makes sense to create and review your mixes and mastered works with that very same apparatus.

While it should now be obvious that you need a pair of headphones for home and mobile-studio use, let's look at some facts that will explain what makes a pair of headphones serious, pro-level cans (see Figure A.3). Knowing and understanding these facts will help soften the blow when you first gaze upon the seemingly inflated price tags you'll encounter when shopping for your first set.

Image courtesy of Ultrasone.

**Figure A.3** After realizing the headphones with the curly connecting cable your Dad has tucked away in a box with his 8-track tape player don't work anymore (did you really think they would?), it's time to consider big-league cans such as these Ultrasone PRO 900 closed-backs.

- One standout difference between headphones is the drivers (see the preceding sidebar on drivers). Pro-level headphones are made with such desirable materials as Mylar, gold-plated Mylar, and even titanium to help deliver pristine reproductions of your productions that are superior to consumer-grade cans.

- Another factor is in the advanced design with regard to driver placement. For instance, the Ultrasones seen in Figure A.3 have their drivers placed slightly below your ear and angled away from your eardrum as opposed to sitting in the center of the earcup. This helps decrease the sound pressure level (SPL) by up to 40 percent, enabling you to work longer and safer.

- Speaking of safety: Pro-level headphones feature shielding to cut down on low-frequency magnetic fields, which can be associated with ailments ranging from fatigue to serious disease.

These factors, along with better overall construction for longer-lasting performance and the use of more comfortable materials on the parts that actually touch your head and ears, contribute to the price of big-league cans. With proper care on your part, what seems like a sizable investment will be a sound and smart one that you need to carefully consider.

---

**Open-Back Versus Closed-Back**   When you're looking into a pair of headphones, there are two basic design types to consider: open-back and closed-back. Open-back phones sport a grill (see Figure A.4) on the outer shell that exposes the driver and allows sound waves to escape the enclosure. That's not necessarily a bad thing; open-back headphones are less susceptible to distortion caused by earcup resonances and allow

Image courtesy of Ultrasone.

**Figure A.4**   Taking a look on the outer shell of the earcup, you'll be able to easily tell whether a pair of headphones is open-back. Just look for a circular series of openings known as a grill, as seen on this pair of Ultrasone HFI-2400s.

sound waves to propagate away from your skull, making for a safer listening experience (see the next sidebar). Of course those propagating waves will be heard by anyone in the general vicinity, so some of the respectful isolation that headphones provide is compromised with open backs. Open backs also afford you the ability to hear what's going on around you, which can be a good thing or a bad thing.

Closed-back headphones, on the other hand, have no grill (refer to Figure A.3) and instead have a sealed backing, which aids in cutting down the amount of audio heard by others as well as isolating your ears from what's going on around you. Just as the open-backs are a give-and-take situation, so are the closed-backs: The isolation you take back gives way to possible earcup resonance producing distortion, but at the same time you get increased bass response.

---

**Warning from the Author General**   Put simply, if you listen to loud sounds in your headphones for prolonged periods of time, your listening days will quickly come to an end—or, if they don't come to an end, you'll surely acquire a problem such as tinnitus, a constant ringing in your ears that will rob you of ever having a truly quiet moment in your life and can cause a barrage of migraines. Trust me, as I write this, I can hear the ringing, now as I have for nearly 20 years. Not fun. To help keep things in check, remember these numbers:

- **85dB SPL:** Around this range is the maximum level recommended for extended exposure.

- **120dB SPL:** This is where things start to get dangerous; it's considered the threshold of pain.

- **130dB SPL:** If you are exposed to this or a higher decibel, it could be game over, as this could result in significant and/or permanent hearing loss.

Please, be careful.

**Microphones**

While many artists work with loop-based, pre-recorded, or MIDI-generated material, there will always be a need for recording real-world sounds. To do this, you will need a microphone or two (or more). In this section, we'll take a look at the main types as well as some common applications so you can get an idea of what mics you may require for whatever it is you're looking to do with your studio.

First, it's important to understand some basic principles. A microphone is a device that transduces (change of one form of energy into another) sound waves (acoustic energy) into a voltage-based signal (electric energy). The transduction works via magnetism (this will be explained in the following two sections). A mic's job is to *hear* or capture whatever sound is within its proximity and transform that sound into voltages that will travel through the connecting mic cable (called an XLR cable) to your audio interface. As you may know, those voltages, which are analogous to the real-world sound waves, are then converted into digital audio in the form of binary code (there's those zeroes and ones again) by the ADC converter. In the end, if you're looking to make music from scratch, then you'll definitely need some good mics. So let's get informed.

### A Microphone READ ME

Because talking about microphones opens a sizeable Pandora's box that includes myriad miking techniques, polar patterns, impedance matching, and more, this section is going to get right to the heart of the matter by exploring three major types of mics: the dynamic, the condenser, and a type of condenser known as an electret. We'll consider how each mic type works and why you might choose to use one type over another. Be aware: There are plenty more types, such as ribbon, piezoelectric, carbon, fiber-optic, PZM, and so on, but it is the three types described in this section that you'll find most useful in the beginning.

> **Note:** For more in-depth information on recording techniques that involve microphones, please visit the Course Technology website (www.courseptr.com) and peruse the Music Technology section. There, you'll find titles that thoroughly examine this technology, any of which will be fine companions to this book.

### Dynamic Mics

If there's one type of microphone you'll definitely need in your studio, it's a dynamic mic. A dynamic microphone consists of a diaphragm attached to a small movable induction coil that's situated in a permanent magnetic field provided by an internal magnet. All these components are located at the top of the mic, inside a component called the capsule. As sound waves enter the capsule, they cause the diaphragm to move, causing the coil to move within the magnetic field. The coil's movements within the magnetic field produce the aforementioned voltages. Dynamic mics are preferred in many instances because their design allows you to capture signals at very high decibel levels without damage. So if you're miking a Marshall stack, for example, be sure to use a dynamic. When you start shopping for dynamic mics, you'll quickly realize there are a lot to choose from. But there's one model that is found in every studio on Planet Rock: the Shure SM-57 (see Figure A.5)—and for good reason. The Shure SM-57 sounds great in myriad applications (especially when miking guitar amps), they're built to last, and they're affordable (about $100). Get one.

Image courtesy of Shure.

**Figure A.5**   There are some things you just gotta have in your studio, and the Shure SM-57 is one of them. If you only need a mic here and there for various applications or you're buying your first one, it's a good idea to get a durable dynamic mic; the SM-57 is a great choice—and a legendary one at that.

### Condenser Mics

A close second in the ranks of must-have mics is the condenser mic. Known for their warmth, condenser mics are a different animal altogether from their dynamic brethren, beginning with the fact that they require a power source. Like dynamic mic, condensers have a diaphragm, but this one is made up of two plates that hold a fixed charge between them. This charge is provided by the power source (usually called *phantom power*), via a cable or internal battery. The sound waves entering the condenser's capsule cause the sensitive plates to move, thus changing the voltage between them. Condensers sound amazing and are great for recording frequency-rich sources such as vocals and acoustic guitars. For even better results, look for condensers that are designed with an internal vacuum tube (as seen in Figure A.6), which add warmth and clarity to the sounds they capture. While condenser mics are fairly rugged as compared to some others, they can't take the same punishment dynamic mics can.

**Figure A.6** Condenser mics are known for their warmth and clarity and are an essential part of any recording studio. The vacuum tube–loaded M-Audio Sputnik seen here is an example of a next-level condenser that comes with its own separate phantom-power source as well as a shock mount, 7-pin cable, and flight case.

### Electret Mics

A type of condenser mic, the electret microphone, has a constant charge between the plates, eliminating the need for phantom power. Another part of their charm is that electrets are quite small compared to their phantom-dependant siblings, making them perfect accessories for high-quality hand-held recording devices such as the M-Audio MicroTrack II (see Figure A.7). When it comes to gathering unique audio content for your studio, you'll quickly get addicted to the world of "found sounds," where you set out into the world and literally hunt, gather, record, and assemble your own sound library. What better way to capture this type of audio than by using one of these compact recording solutions equipped with a great-sounding condenser mic? The entire recording outfit can fit in your pocket!

### Microphone Controls

When it comes to working with microphones, there are some controls you'll run into on both the mics themselves and the devices they're patched into—audio interface and/or mixing console—that you should be aware of when

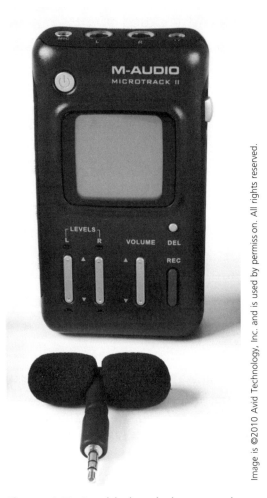

**Figure A.7**  Double-headed stereo electret mics (such as the one at the forefront) are a great-sounding compact solution that perfectly complement high-quality mobile-recording devices such as this M-Audio Micro Track II.

starting to build your arsenal. They are listed in the order you'll most likely have to deal with them. They are as follows:

- **Phantom power.** As stated in the section on condenser mics, phantom power is needed to provide a fixed charge between the plates that make up the mic's diaphragm. You'll find a button marked "phantom power," 48 v (v = volts), or the like on your audio interface and/or mixing console (see Figure A.8) for mics that require it. (Along with electrets that do not require phantom power, some condensers work on batteries.) If you know you're going to be using a condenser for recording, be sure to activate the phantom power function *before* you connect the mic to prevent any sudden pops in the system that could damage your monitors. That said, also make sure the master volume on

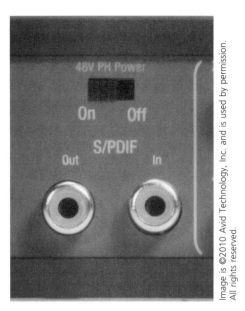

**Figure A.8**   When using a condenser mic that requires a fixed charge provided by the device it's connected to, you'll need to locate the switch to turn it on. The one shown here is found on the rear of the previously examined M-Audio Fast Track Pro.

your interface is all the way down. This is a good habit to get into whenever switching any hardware in and out of your system.

- **Polar pattern.** This is a function that sets up the mic's directionality in relation to the capsule. While most dynamic mics are only capable of one polar pattern, if the mic is a multi-pattern unit, this control will be in the form of a small switch (see Figure A.9) that will have small icons shaped like the patterns offered. The most common polar pattern is cardioid, but other useful patterns are omni-directional and bi-directional (see Figure A.9 for a visual reference of all three patterns). If you need the mic to specifically hone in on a source, then use a cardioid-type pattern. (There are also hyper- and super-cardioid patterns, which offer more acute directionality.) If you need a mic to simultaneously record from its opposing sides, then engage the bi-directional pattern (also known as

**Figure A.9**   If a mic offers more than one polar pattern, you'll be able to choose which one you want to use by way of a tiny switch that's adorned with images of the patterns offered, like with this Audio-Technica AT4047MP multi-pattern condenser. The patterns shown here are as follows: omni-directional, cardioid, and bi-directional.

figure-eight). For focusing on everything around the capsule, omni-directional is the way to go.

- **Pad.** This is a device that can be found not only on microphones (see Figure A.10) but also on audio interfaces and mixing consoles. In all cases, a pad attenuates (decreases) an incoming signal that is too hot (loud) for the device to handle. Pads usually come in the form of −10 or −20dB. Word to the wise: Before you go flipping the pad switch whenever the red light flashes, consider whether the source needs to be that loud or whether the microphone is placed too close to the source.

Image courtesy of Georg Neumann GmbH.

**Figure A.10**   If the signal coming into your system is too hot to handle, you can engage a pad that is either located on the mic itself as seen on the legendary Neumann U 87 Ai or the device the mic is connected to.

- **Bass roll-off.** A simple function, but an essential one nonetheless, a bass roll-off (see Figure A.11) simply cuts off a mic's frequency response below a certain cutoff frequency (usually 80Hz) and comes especially handy when recording vocals. This control is usually a small, two-position toggle switch with an icon at each end of the switch's throw indicating flat response (straight line) or roll-off (straight line with a downward slope at the end toward the right side). This is useful when the source you're recording has some sonic qualities that produce low frequencies that prove to be too much to capture without muddying up the take or there's simply a rumble in the range of the mic's polar pattern not caused by the source itself that cannot be eliminated. Another instance where a roll-off is a great quick fix is when you're faced with the *proximity effect*, in which a mic's placement causes a sudden increase in the low range. While simply moving the mic will most likely solve the problem, that may also result in losing a great sound that just needs some slight attenuation (decrease) in the bottom end.

Image of courtesy of Electro-Voice.

**Figure A.11** A bass roll-off switch, as seen on the venerable Sennheiser RE-20, is a great quick fix for low-end problems. This reserved-looking control is usually identified by two basic images that a second-grader could draw.

## MIDI Controllers

I covered MIDI controllers briefly in Chapter 1, but they warrant more discussion here. Here, we will take a look at some more hardware MIDI controller options, such as the Akai APC40 and the Novation Launchpad.

When it comes to MIDI controllers, the song remains the same: As your studio, knowledge, and audio-production skills develop, so will your MIDI hardware preferences. What is the absolute must-have MIDI piece for your production needs today may be something completely different a year from now. That said, don't think you have to spend a lot of time planning your musical future; you can't. Nor can you know what controller will be perfect for you. You just have to follow where your muse takes you. Once you get your head around the sheer power that MIDI sequencing and hardware controllers offer, you'll see why there is so much emphasis put on them in the music culture. Finally, be warned: Once you get a gander at what's available, you're gonna want it *all*. Here is just a taste to whet your appetite.

### Mixer-Style Controllers

Prior to computers, the center of any recording studio was the mixing console (see Figure A.12), where (almost) total control of all aspects of the recording and mixing process was at your fingertips. While mixers are very much still a vital part of the recording studio and its activities, the computer, as well as digital audio workstation (DAW) software, has stolen its thunder in recent years. The primary purpose of these hardware wonders was/is *mixing*, which refers to combining multiple audio components into a final product whose volume levels and frequency content have been

Image courtesy of Mackie.

**Figure A.12**   At the center of many recording studios of all levels is the mighty mixing console.

adjusted for an optimum listening experience. For the most part, volume adjustments are made with track faders, and frequency-related tweaks are done with knobs. Of course, this is a gross generalization, but an accurate one nonetheless.

Seeing that we're building your studio, a good first MIDI controller would be an affordable mixer-style unit that has the feel of an analog mixer but communicates with your DAW and your computer through MIDI, such as the ultra-compact Korg Nano Kontrol (see Figure A.13). Featuring nine faders, nine knobs, and 18 buttons, as well as transport controls that can be assigned to tweak anything that requires the twist of an encoder, you can comfortably control your DAW with minimal use of the mouse. If you've already been toying with your DAW via a mouse, you'll quickly come to appreciate not having to rely on it for everything.

Image courtesy of Korg.

**Figure A.13**   While there are no signs of putting analog mixers to pasture, it's now the norm to have some type of mixer-style MIDI controller in your studio setup, especially if you're mobile to some degree.

### Keyboard Controllers

Those who suffer from GAS (gear-acquisition syndrome) will be pleased to know it's not uncommon to have more than one MIDI controller. At the very least, you'll need one mixer-style controller and one keyboard-style controller in your studio. Keyboard-centric controllers such as the M-Audio Keystation 61es (see Figure A.14) work great when you want to actually play the data you need to input into a MIDI track.

**Figure A.14** Right up there on, if not at the top of, the list of MIDI controllers is a bare-bones keyboard-style controller that allows you to actually play MIDI performances into a MIDI track as well as perform other tasks like triggering samples, such as this M-Audio Keystation 61es.

Now, don't let the keyboard aspect of it throw you. There's more to be played than just keyboard parts. Capturing MIDI data through performance started out on keyboards and that meant any sound, or rather *synthesized* sound, was "played" on them. If you're looking at a compromised desktop real-estate situation or just want to consolidate hardware, there are plenty of compact keyboard-style controllers that feature mixer-like controls such as knobs, sliders (closely related to faders), and more, including the delicious-looking Novation SL Mk II (see Figure A.15).

**Figure A.15** If space constraints are a concern, consider a hybrid mixer/keyboard–style unit like the Novation SL Mk II. With its array of encoders, knobs, and sliders, the SL Mk II can cover a lot of ground without taking too much of it.

### *Percussion-Style Controllers*

While inputting data with keys on a piano/synth–style keyboard controller will work great for myriad scenarios including drum sequencing, some may find having a controller that's more percussion-centric better suited for beat making. Controllers such as the Akai MPD 18 (see Figure A.16) feature touch-sensitive trigger pads that feel more natural when inputting data percussively.

**Figure A.16**    MIDI controllers such as this compact Akai MPD 18 feature touch-sensitive pads that are perfect for beat production as well as triggering.

Stepping up from trigger pads and inputting data with your fingertips, there are percussion-style controllers that are designed with larger pads, allowing you to hit them with sticks, such as the Yamaha DTX-Multi 12. While controllers like the MPD 18 or M-Audio's venerable Trigger Finger can be seen on plenty of stages, it's controllers like the DTX-Multi 12 or the legendary DrumKAT that will come in handy for drummers who have some chops to burn. With regard to sound production, it's important to note the Yamaha unit also makes some noise of its own, with more than 1,000 built-in voices among other attributes. In the spirit of desktop economy, go back and take another look at the Novation SL Mk II in Figure A.15, and you'll see a line of eight pads on the left right above the joystick controller.

### Instrument-Style Controllers

Taking the performance aspect of MIDI controllers beyond the standard keyboard- and percussion-style controllers, there are MIDI devices modeled after other real-world instruments. For instance, if you're a drummer and you want even more than what the aforementioned percussion-style controllers offer, then check out one of the Roland V-Drum kits (see Figure A.17). Also featuring major sound-producing capabilities, every V-Drum kit is equipped to send out not only audio through its sound module but also MIDI performance data for you to work with in Live.

Image courtesy of Roland.

**Figure A.17**  While controllers that feature touch-sensitive pads provide a great way to produce beats with MIDI, if you're a drummer, a kit like one of the Roland V-Drums setups may be exactly what you're looking for.

For guitarists, there are some eye-catching instrument-style controllers to fuss over, like the too-cool Misa Digital Guitar (see Figure A.18) with its innovative touch-screen LCD or one of Starr Labs' Ztar guitar-like MIDI controllers. If you're too attached to your own axe, then just throw on a Roland GK-3 Divided Pickup (see Figure A.19) and interface with either compatible synth modules or a Roland GI-20 (see Figure A.20) to send raw MIDI to wherever you want. There are even options for horn players, with the groundbreaking EWI (electronic wind instrument) USB from Akai (see Figure A.21).

Image courtesy of Misa.

**Figure A.18**  If you're a guitarist with iPod Touch or Korg Kaoss Pad chops, you'll be excited about the Misa Digital Guitar for your diabolical MIDI-driven creations and/or performances.

Image courtesy of Roland.

**Figure A.19**  For the guitar purist, there's a MIDI solution that will allow you to play the old wood 'n steel. By using a non-invasive add-on hex pickup like this Roland GK-3, you can set up a rig that allows you to play a conventional guitar and have each string's vibration individually picked up and sent off to a pitch-to-MIDI converter. From there, your guitar signal is converted into digital in the form of MIDI messages and functions much the same as any other MIDI controller.

### DJ-Style Controllers

Given the fact that the digital DJ has long-since arrived and live dance music is hotter than ever, it should come as no surprise that there are plenty of DJ-style controllers to choose from, including delicious-looking units from usual and not-so-usual suspects. These include the following:

- Native Instruments
- M-Audio

Image courtesy of Roland.

**Figure A.20**   The Roland GI-20 is the go-to pitch-to-MIDI converter. If you're using a hex pickup like the GK-3 (see Figure A.19), you would use a 13-pin connector cable to connect the pickup to the GI-20 so the separated analog signals can travel into the unit for conversion.

Image courtesy of Akai.

**Figure A.21**   Instrument-style controllers extend as far as wind instruments, as seen here with the game-changing Akai EWI USB.

- Allen & Heath (see Figure A.22)
- Denon
- Numark
- Rane
- Pioneer
- Vestax

With a crossfader being the prime giveaway that a unit is Jam Master Jay–ready (the pro-Ableton Akai APC40 being a notable exception), DJ-style controllers feature a double-sided array of controls such as knobs, faders, buttons, and whatever else it takes for the user to get that party started.

Image courtesy of Allen & Heath.

**Figure A.22**   DJ-style MIDI controllers offer the same double-sided control interface as traditional analog controllers plus a whole lot more. Some even come equipped with jog wheels for scratch-like maneuvers, like the pair perched in the lower corners of this Allen & Heath Xone:4D.

### Grid-Based and Hybrid-Grid–Based Controllers

There are a number of grid-based controllers available, with perhaps the most capable being the Akai APC40 and Novation Launchpad (see Figures A.23 and A.24).

There are a handful of controllers that offer a completely different way to approach working and performing. While there are controllers that feature an array of mostly (if not all) buttons such as the Faderfox LX2, the key component is its visual-feedback aspect. Grid-based controllers are designed for bi-directional talkback, which simply means the device not

Image courtesy of Akai Professional.

**Figure A.23**   At the heart of the all-encompassing APC40 is a 5×8 grid of soft buttons that can be used for clip triggering, among many other applications. For a more desktop–real-estate friendly version, check out the 40's little brother, the APC20.

Image courtesy of Novation. Copyright © Focusrite Audio Engineering Limited 2011.

**Figure A.24**  The Novation Launchpad is all about the grid.

only sends messages to the software it's controlling but also receives them. This allows MIDI messages to be sent to the controller that instructs the button grid to light up in myriad ways, making for an incredible interactive experience. Some other examples are the Flame Six-In-A-Row, the Livid Block, and of course any one of the pioneering Monome units.

### "Other" Controllers

For the adventurous, there is a handful of cool controllers that defy category, from innovative touch-screen controls like the Lemur by JazzMutant, to the perplexing AudioCubes from Percussa, to the near-genius DIY creations like the Mojo (see Figure A.25).

Image courtesy of Rory Earnshaw Photography.

**Figure A.25**  If you can't beat 'em, build your own! That's exactly what controllerism pioneer Moldover did when he just couldn't find a controller that had all the attributes he desired in one unit—not to mention features that no manufacturer was offering. After creating his fair share of Frankenstein controllers through hacking, he designed the Mojo controller. Tricked out with top-shelf arcade buttons, a plethora of ribbon controls, and faders arranged in the shape of the human hand, the Mojo is a feat of human excellence and one cool MIDI controller.

## The Little Things

At this point, the core components of your studio have been revealed (and possibly obtained by you). Although you can surely go ahead and start getting your hands dirty in setup procedures, there's a truckload of little things you will need sooner or later as you start to work in your newfound studio environment. The following sections feature numerous items—enough to make your head explode—accompanied by short descriptions.

### Cables

To connect all this gear, you will need cables—a lot of them. Aside from the obvious ¼-inch tipped types, there are myriad cables that will see action in your studio—albeit some more than others. As you slowly gather this spaghetti army, you might think, "Do I really need all these?" The short answer is, *yes!*

A good way to establish your cable collection is to gather them as you go along. For instance, you don't necessarily need a 75-ohm coaxial S/PDIF cable or its TOSLink brethren just yet. When you do, get one. And after you do so, *save it*. If Murphy's Law has its way, the day you clean house and get rid of all those cables you never use, you can bet you'll be wishing you hadn't in the not-so-distant future (the next day) when a situation arises that needs that not-so-common cable you just snickered at as you sold it for a $1 at a yard sale.

Try not to go running for the cheapies to stock your pile. Stick with names like Hosa (see the upcoming sidebar) and ProCo in the beginning, and you'll be okay. As your studio (and ears) develops, you can upgrade as you progress. All that said, the following list comprises, in no particular order, the cabling you must have to get your studio off the ground.

- **Computer cables.** Be they USB or FireWire, it's always a good idea to have multiples of each in varying lengths in a computer-based music-production studio. And that goes for the various types of each cable, such as USB cables that feature smaller connectors and FireWire cables that work with the different transfer types (that is, FW400 and FW800).

- **¼-inch instrument.** The ¼-inch cable is the most common audio cable. It comes in two basic types: TS and TRS. The pointed end is called the tip (T). Below the tip is a small black ring that separates it from the sleeve (S), which is the shaft that makes up the remainder of the jack. A jack with one black ring can be called a TS cable, although it's usually known as a "¼-inch" or "instrument" cable. These cable types feature a single conductor (connected to the tip, while the sleeve is the ground) and are used to connect one device to another in mono. If the jack has two plastic black rings, it's a TRS (tip-ring-sleeve) cable. For the most part, these cable types also carry a mono signal, but one that is *balanced*. The extra ring is connected to a second conductor whose polarity is reversed, which provides a means for unwanted noise cancellation when running long cable lengths and/or exposing the cable to noisy electrical fields. Then you have some form of a tip-ring-sleeve (TRS) with the middle portion being the ring and the outer portions following the nomenclature just explained. These types of ¼-inch cables can also be used for carrying stereo signals (one channel per conductor) or for carrying two signals in opposite directions (one direction per conductor). Be sure you know which type of TRS you're working with, as using the wrong one will result in varying degrees of failure.

- **Speaker.** These cable types are designed to connect your monitoring systems to whatever device is last in the signal chain that's passing the audio along. They come in three different connector types: ¼-inch, banana plug, and Neutrik Speakon, with ¼-inch being the most common. Given that fact, it's very important not to mistakenly mix speaker and instrument cables (more so with speaker cable being used as instrument cable, as this will produce a lot of noise). More times than not, ¼-inch cables of all types are marked as such near the jacks right near the sleeve

- **XLR.** These are the cables you use to connect any microphone worth its salt to its destination device. XLR cables always have a male and female end that always make the same connection. The female end is the one that plugs into the mic itself, while the male end always plugs into the connecting device such as an audio interface, mixing console, or snake. You can never have enough XLR cables, and it's a smart move to have them in varying lengths. If you need an extraordinarily long XLR, you can always connect two of them together!

- **Patch cords.** If you'll be using outboard processors and/or a patch bay, you'll quickly appreciate the existence of compact ¼-inch cables known as patch cables. Usually coming in bulk packages in an array of colors, these cables are similar to instrument cables with the noticeable difference being they range from a few inches to a foot in length.

- **MIDI.** Cables with a round, hollow connector that have five pins inside are the ones used for connecting MIDI devices. Unlike XLR connections, there are no female MIDI connectors, only male ends that connect into the female jacks on all MIDI-compatible gear.

- **RCA.** If you partake in modern media at even the most elementary level, you've come across RCA cables—the rounded-end cables that connect most every piece of consumer-level A/V equipment, including your stereo and entertainment system. You'll find these plug types on audio interfaces in the form of main outs and on DJ mixers to connect turntables, to name a few. With regard to the former, they're considered a lower-grade connection system as they are unbalanced and thus susceptible to noise and interference, but at the same time they help keep costs down and are usually used on more compact units.

This list is by no means complete; you'll likely work with several other types of cables over the course of your music-making career. But these are the essentials. When it comes to cost, it may not be within your budget nor your immediate needs to get the best of the best, but try not to be too prudent, as cheap cables are just that. They will deliver sub-par results and will fail much sooner than higher-quality ones.

## Adapters

For every cable listed above, if there's an adapter available to convert one type to another, *get it!* Make that two, because you *will* lose them and/or they'll grow legs and walk out of your studio. Dedicate a drawer to these items so you'll always know where they are. Following is a list of a few adapters that will surely come up much sooner than later. Take note: When viewing the list, think "vice versa" on the adapters that are displayed as *x*-to-*x*.

- **¼-inch-to-⅛-inch.** There are many cabling scenarios that use the smaller ⅛-inch jack (also known as 3.5 mm, while ¼-inch jacks are 6.35 mm); these adapters are used to make the larger ¼-inch types fit into the smaller plugs. Make sure out of the two types—mono and stereo—you have multiple stereo adapters, as these will be used way more often. Most commonly used for making sure your headphone jack will connect with whatever device you need to plug into, if you don't have one of these adapters and have headphones that have the opposite jack, that late-night session is toast if you have a home studio that's not substantially soundproofed.

- **Low-Z/High-Z.** That's the nickname for an adapter that serves as an impedance (Z) transformer that is one part female XLR (Low Z) and one part TS ¼-inch (High Z). These are great for when you just have to connect an XLR cable into a ¼-inch jack. At the same time, try not to find yourself in this scenario unless it's completely unavoidable, as it delivers compromised results.

- **USB adapters.** The rectangular end of a USB cable is called Type A, and it's always the connection needed to plug into the computer itself. It's the other end that has variables that may call for an adapter. The almost squared-off Type B connector is the most commonly used type to plug into the devices that are being patched into your computer. But there are alternative, smaller mini- and micro-type connectors for, well, smaller devices. For example, the compact Korg Nano Kontrol (refer to Figure A.13) discussed back in the "MIDI Controllers" section uses the more compact Mini-A connector.

- **RCA-to-¼-inch.** There will be plenty of times when you look to see what the connection type is on a piece of hardware (probably an interface) and you'll discover it's RCA instead of the expected ¼-inch. This adapter will save the day (and save you from having to schlep to the music store, wasting precious studio time).

- **Y-adapters.** If you have an instance where stereo signals are involved but one of the devices has only one stereo plug, you may need a Y-adapter of some type. Aptly named, these adapters have two separate wires that come together into one jack. They could be two RCA female to one ¼-inch male or two ¼-inch female to one ⅛-inch male. There are many possibilities, but if you had to start somewhere, these two are safe bets.

---

**Hosa Frijoles**   When it comes to adapters and many other accessories (including cables) for your studio, it's hard to find a more comprehensive solution than Hosa. Simply put, these guys make *everything*. In adapters alone, you'll be hard pressed to *not* find what you're looking for when perusing their website (www.hosatech.com). In fact, you may not need to, as most any pro audio store or even local guitar shop will stock Hosa products in great numbers.

---

**Odds and Ends**

If you're starting to think this list will never end, you're right—it won't! Just remember: The more you put into your studio, the greater the return. When you have the goods to make your music come to life, it makes all the time, effort, and investment more than worth it. Before we close things out with some furniture talk, here's a quick list of some odds and ends that every studio should have. Many of these items are inexpensive and probably won't exceed $200 (excluding the DIs, bulk orders of gaffer's tape, and refrigerator), but are no less important than the "big" purchases.

- **Stands.** Make sure you not only have mic stands but music stands as well. With regard to the latter, it's not always a matter of reading music per se, but a matter of having somewhere to put notes, lyrics, pictures, and so on. You never know what you or someone you're working with will need to make the magic happen.

- **Mic clips.** Most mic stands *do not* come with the clamp-type apparatus known as a clip that's used to hold the microphone in place. While some mics come with their own proprietary clips and shock mounts, a handful of generic clips are a must.

- **Batteries.** At the top of the list are 9-volt batteries, with AA being a close second. You may not see too many instances of the other types, but it never hurts to have a small quantity of C, D, and AAAs in the drawer (with a slight emphasis on AAAs).

- **Sharpies.** These markers are great for writing on myriad surfaces, especially CDs and DVDs. You'll often need to jot down a quick description after burning a fresh copy of your latest mix.

- **Gaffer's tape.** Hands down, a studio must. Whether it be for taping cables down to ensure no one will trip on them or taping down adapters in a surge protector, gaffer's tape is *the* go-to studio tape because it holds incredibly well while leaving almost no residue when you remove it.

- **Refrigerator.** Depending on where your studio is located, (or, if it's in your house, like most project studios, how far it is from the kitchen), you may need to invest in a small fridge. During long, tedious editing sessions or taxing tracking sessions, it's a good idea to have liquids nearby so you can keep yourself hydrated. While you're at it, stocking that mini-fridge with some fruit and other high-energy food is a smart move as well.

- **DI boxes.** When plugging an instrument directly into an audio interface and/or mixing console, you will need what's called a direct box, or DI for short (which stands for direct input). This allows you to connect a high-impedance, line-level, and/or unbalanced incoming signal to a low-impedance, microphone-level input that is balanced—the most common scenario being a ¼-inch source going into the DI and an XLR cable coming out to the destination device of choice. And, don't get just one!

- **Blank CDs/DVDs.** A spool of at least 50 of each should be on hand at all times.

- **Tuner.** Never depend on someone else to have a tuner. While many virtual modeling apps feature built-in tuners, nothing beats the convenience of a portable hardware tuner to quickly plug into. Try to get one with a big, bright LCD so you can use it live, too.

- **Metronome.** While most DAWs have their own built-in metronome, having a standalone will come in handy when you need one and your DAW is busy doing something else (rendering, for instance). Make sure whatever one you choose has a tap tempo function where you can tap a pulse to reveal a tempo.

- **Strings/picks.** No matter what type of music you'll be producing, a guitar and bass will surely be involved at some point. Aside from breaking strings and having to be forced to replace them on an as-needed basis, a fresh set of strings can be exactly what a lifeless-sounding guitar track could use. As for picks, they're just like adapters: They grow legs. Also, different picks have different tonal properties and afford different techniques. Get a handful of varying types to have on hand.

## Home Studio Furnishings

This section discusses some preliminary studio furnishings to add to the must-have list. If you've even acquired a quarter of what has been discussed thus far, you've already realized that the coffee table you were thinking of resurrecting from the garage isn't going to cut it—not by a long shot—and neither will that folding chair the catering company left at your house after that high-school–graduation party your family had a few years ago. What's more, you will soon be building a sizable collection of myriad ancillary items discussed in the previous section (many of which are pretty darned small and therefore easily lost) that need an organized place to live. Strongly consider the following three items as you scope out your studio's location in the next chapter.

## The Workstation

Your studio will really start to take shape when you have its centerpiece in place: the workstation. Similar to a home computer desk in philosophy, a workstation (see Figure A.26) is an ergonomic, highly functional piece furniture specifically designed for music-studio needs. While these units have the prerequisite desktop space, a pullout tray for your computer keyboard, and multiple tiers for placing various hardware such as your tower and monitors, the similarities end there. Taking it to the next level, music workstations offer the following features to make your studio environment that much more effective:

- **Expanded shelving.** As you'll soon see, there's a great deal of strategy that goes into what goes where with regard to smooth workflow and, more importantly, sonic projection. A good workstation should provide ample shelving and desktop real estate for placing your core hardware—computers monitor(s), studio monitors, MIDI control surface and/or

Image courtesy of Omnirax Technical Furniture.

**Figure A.26**  At the center of it all, the workstation will be where you make the magic happen. Make sure you go for a station designed specifically for music production, such as this Omnirax Force 36. From expanded shelving and compartments to casters allowing you to move your world around the room at will, you'll be thankful you made the investment in the seemingly insignificant category.

keyboard controller, and so on—in places where you can work most comfortably while at the same time allowing you to place components such as monitors in positions where they're most effective for a discerning listening environment. In addition, you're going to need many items at close hand as you work no matter what the project calls for. These items need to be within arm's reach without cluttering your workspace. Be sure to map out what you think you will need to live on the workstation so you can make a smart, informed decision when pondering this important purchase. While you're at it, look for a piece of furniture that is a bit more than you need and affords you room to grow. You will, and that's a fact—albeit a fun one.

- **Rackbays.** At some point, your studio will surely include a few (if not many) pieces of outboard processors, often called "rack gear." The reason for this nickname can be found on the front panel of these powerful rectangular DSP units, where there are winged extensions, or ears, on both sides that are used for mounting (see Figure A.27). Any workstation worth its wheels will have at least a pair of two-space rackbays for mounting these processors, making for convenient positioning. In case you're wondering whether the rack piece you have or will obtain will fit into the rackbays, no worries. The dimensions for *all* outboard processors of this ilk are a standard 19-inch wide, and the mounting slots are guaranteed to line up with the workstations.

Image courtesy of Furman.

**Figure A.27**  To mount any outboard rack gear to your workstation's rackbay, each component will have a pair of rack ears—one on each side, as seen on this Furman M-8Dx power conditioner—whose mounting slots will perfectly match up with the bay's slots.

- **Advanced wire management.** When it comes to cables, if you build it (that is, your studio), they will come. It's a good idea to organize your wires right from the beginning. Fortunately, your workstation can provide several means in which to do so. Below each rackbay and other smartly placed locations, you'll find cabling *grommets* (see Figure A.28),

**Figure A.28** When shopping for your workstation, make sure the desk has small plastic circular grommets wherever there will be wires of any kind, to ensure tidy cabling.

which are plastic cylindrical pieces used for wire management that are meant to fit snuggly into circular cuts made into the desktop area and/or side walls. On more involved workstations, you may also find larger openings in the back walls that are meant for larger bundles of cabling. These openings will also have some sort of plastic border such as PVC T-molding to cut down on any chances the wires may become damaged due to hanging over potentially sharp wood edges that may cut into a cable's outer casing.

- **Sturdy construction.** The combination of computer hardware, rack gear, MIDI gear, a mixing console, and more will be hefty in weight to say the least. A dedicated music workstation should be built with sturdy materials such as furniture-grade oak plywood to ensure a long-lasting existence. The station may also be covered with high-pressure laminate surfaces such as thermo-fused melamine or Formica so that it can best take on the punishment you will surely dish out on the desktop and shelving areas as you work.

- **Casters.** There may be times when you'll need to move things around in your studio. Be it an impromptu live recording session or a mixdown that calls for some extra gear—say, an old analog ½-inch tape machine to warm things up—you may need to rearrange your room's current setup. Luckily for you, most workstations come equipped with appropriately weighted casters (wheels), allowing you to easily roll the apex of your studio wherever you need it to go.

## The Captain's Chair

Think of your studio as a complex vessel that you alone are the captain of. It is you who commands this Enterprise from top to bottom—and considering the sizable investment involved, it is you who will go down with her if she sinks!

Naturally, every captain, including James Tiberius Kirk, has a chair in which they alone rest their bottom, and so should you. Kidding aside, your chair is a huge deal. Think about it: No one piece of gear in your studio will be used more. It will be the first apparatus you go for upon entering and the last one you touch before leaving, not to mention the one you will use most when *not* making music. It is in the captain's chair that you will spend countless hours slaving over your creations, so take this search seriously. When setting sail for the ultimate studio chair, keep these thoughts at the bow of you brain:

- At the top of all considerations should be comfort. Do not settle for anything less than perfect. Make sure there's ample back support, too. Remember: Only you can make this call. Unless you can sit in the chair your forum buddy swears is the best, don't even think about ordering a chair online sight un-sat! Trying it before buying it is of paramount importance.

- It has to be adjustable. The more options, the better.

- Absolutely no noise can emanate from your chair—at least any that you determine cannot be eliminated with a quick spray of WD-40.

- Mobility in the form being able to spin freely (with no squeaks, of course) and being able to smoothly glide across the room on the casters is a big one.

- If you play an instrument, especially a fretted one like a guitar or bass, make sure you can remove any arms that you think may impede playing of said axes.

While there do exist dedicated manufacturers of chairs designed for studio use such as Bob Hall & Company (they make the MusicComfort Studio model), a trip to any one of the major office retailers such as Staples or OfficeMax will do the trick. Usually set up in the back, you'll find upwards of 30 different chairs of all sizes and shapes assembled for your seating pleasure. What's more, you'll most likely get the best deal going, finding a chair around $100 give or take a few dollars. Be sure to make the journey during a time when you know the store will be empty to ensure you can sit on every last chair, multiple times, while at the same time minimizing the inevitable stares you *will* attract as you air-position yourself in music-studio mode.

**Organizers**

Before you know it, your studio is going to be inundated with stuff. You name it: computers, speakers, cables, guitars, mics, McDonald's—everything. Though it may be hard to predict exactly what you'll need, it's a good idea to budget in a series of organizing apparatuses such as the following:

- **Shelves.** You're going to accumulate countless items of medium size—controllers, guitar effects, headphones, sample CDs, manuals, and of course Course Technology PTR texts including this book, to name a few —that will need a place to go when not in use. Standalone pieces of furniture and/or wall-mounted types will do just fine and help clear the studio of unnecessary clutter resulting from very necessary things that have nowhere to go.

- **Storage containers.** Just take a quick trip to the nearest Target or any major retailer that stocks home goods and you will have an incredible array of storage containers before you. From pieces that feature stacks of removable, skinny drawers with flip-tops to massive tubs you can probably sleep in—you'll be hard pressed *not* to find a container to fit your needs.

- **Incidental wall-mounted items.** Be it hooks, a dry-erase board, or something as simple as thumb tacks to hang a calendar as opposed to having one sitting on your workstation desktop, burglarizing precious space, elevating miscellaneous items in your studio will organize things greatly. As an added bonus, they may provide some cost-effective room treatments to combat common sound-wave challenges that are inherent with four-walled enclosures.

- **Filing cabinet.** With a studio comes a paper trail composed of warranty cards, manuals, receipts, charts, and yes, take-out menus. Having a filing cabinet is so elementary, you just might overlook obtaining one. Don't.

At this point, there may be what seems like an overabundance of cardboard gathering at your front doorstep thanks to frequent visits from the UPS guy. But the local recycling center will thank you for your contribution—and you'll have a well-outfitted studio.

# Appendix B: Interviews with Laura Escudé and Don Hill

---

**Interview with Laura Escudé**

**Could you give us a quick introduction with some of the albums, software packages, and singles you've been a part of?**

Hi, I'm Laura Escudé and I'm a violinist, composer, sound designer, and music technologist. In 2010, I self-released my first solo album, *Pororoca*, through my label, Electronic Creatives. I've been a part of numerous other albums in the past, contributing production and violin work. Some of the artists are Carmen Rizzo, Trace Element, PlatEAU, Sage Francis, and Solillaquists of Sound. I've composed music for Visa and programmed shows for Cirque du Soleil, Kanye West, Drake, and others using Ableton Live. I am an Ableton Certified Trainer and work very closely with Ableton, among others, such as Native Instruments and Rob Papen.

**How much experience have you had with free or open-source music plug-ins?**

Throughout the years, I've always sought out free and open-source music plug-ins to enhance my music. The things that most people think are really obscure can sometimes create interesting, unique sounds that are unlike what you can find in standard plug-ins. One of the main sites that I've frequented is www.smartelectronix.com; I've found lots of good ones on there, including Livecut. Recently I've been into the plug-ins at www.michaelnorris.info. Michael released a suite of all free plug-ins that make great sound-design tools.

**Is there a particular audio plug-in of which you are extremely fond? Feel free to list multiple ones.**

Recently, I've really been into the iZotope/BT collaboration of Stutter Edit. Wow! This plug-in really blows away all of the other "glitch" types of effects out there. I really like the fact that it's MIDI controlled as well, so by playing a keyboard I can go through different presets or effects and not have to go to my mouse to change the preset.

I always tend to go to the Rob Papen suite of plug-ins; I'm really looking forward to his new Punch drum synthesizer, which will be released soon. Rob and I worked on a synthesizer tutorial video, which should be released this year as well.

The Native Instruments Komplete bundle is always a go-to for me. I use Kontakt quite a bit for more film-scoring work and have been digging really deep into Massive for grittier sounds recently. I can pretty much get any type of sound with the Komplete package, and I've got about a zillion Reaktor patches. The community on the NI website is great because there are tons of great, free Reaktor patches for download from brilliant innovators.

**Could you share a quick story about where this plug-in has really shined during your music creation/production work?**

Well, recently, I've been working on a remix for C.C. Sheffield, who is a vocalist. I've been experimenting with Stutter Edit on her vocals, going through the presets and creating my own in order to make the vocals sound really unique. It's extremely fun to use it on vocals to stretch and glitch them out, if only using it sparingly in certain places. It's really added a futuristic element to the song, and I'm looking forward to putting it out there in the world.

**Is there a particular free/open-source virtual instrument of which you've become fond? Feel free to list multiple ones.**

Recently, I've gotten fond of Spectral DroneMaker by Michael Norris. My friend, Brian Trifon of Trifonic, made this excellent tutorial on how to use it: vimeo.com/13059318.

I've been experimenting with it to make some unique pad sounds out of my violin recordings and other samples I have recorded in the past.

**Could you share a quick story about where this instrument has really shined during your music creation/production work?**

Well, recently, I've been working on creating some meditative music for some visualizations that my mom recorded, and I've been using it to create some interesting drone sounds underneath. She's a master certified coach and has seen some really positive feedback from her clients so far.

**Have you had any difficulties installing or working with any of the free/open-source plug-ins that you've checked out?**

I haven't really experienced difficulties installing, but sometimes the plug-ins in different formats don't seem to show up in different software programs—such as Logic, for example. Also, some of them require you to navigate to the Plug-Ins folder on your computer to install, rather than just double-clicking on an installer that places them there. But it's a great thing to know where these plug-ins are located, in case you have a rogue one that you need to remove.

**Do you have any advice for beginner musicians/producers working with free/open-source audio plug-ins?**

Test out different ones and then get rid of those that you won't use. In the past, it seemed like a great idea to collect as many things as possible, but now I'm trying to be more minimalistic and only have installed what I use. Sometimes limiting the tools you can use enhances the creative process.

**Interview with Don Hill/Millipede**

**Could you give us a quick introduction with some of the albums, software packages, and singles you've been a part of?**

My name is Don Hill. I've been involved in electronic music since 1997 under the names Porteur de l'Image and now Millipede. I have three full-length CDs and one net-released EP. (Porteur de l'Image: *Through a Glass Darkly*; Millipede: *All My Best Intentions* and *Powerless* [both on Hymen Records] and *Phi EP* [Flaming Fish Music].) I also have numerous compilation appearances.

**How much experience have you had with free or open-source music plug-ins?**

A lot of the soft synths and effects I use are available for free. Because I don't have much money to play with (my wife and I have three boys), I've mostly used freeware (outside of using Ableton Live as my DAW).

**Is there a particular audio plug-in of which you are extremely fond? Feel free to list multiple ones. And is there a particular free/open-source virtual instrument of which you've become fond? Feel free to list multiple ones.**

Green Oak's Crystal soft synth is an incredibly deep monster! And there are so many patches available that people share in that community. Even if you never get around to learning how to manipulate it, there's plenty to use.

Two of my favorites to combine are TAL's Bassline VSTi and Camel Audio's CamelCrusher combo simulator. Together, they make for a vicious lead synth.

**Could you share a quick story about where this plug-in or instrument has really shined during your music creation/ production work?**

I have a track on the first Millipede CD that is essentially one note from a Crystal patch, re-triggered every eight bars or so. I built the rest of the song around that.

Bassline and CamelCrusher is my go-to setup if I want a strong lead sound. Even if I end up changing it later, it's a great thing to start with and keep ideas moving.

**Have you had any difficulties installing or working with any of the free/open-source plug-ins that you've checked out?**

The biggest difficulty I've ever had is a couple of years ago with Pluggo-based effects. They tended to be very temperamental or just didn't work at all. It could easily have been my own ignorance, but I never had luck with them.

**Do you have any advice for beginner musicians/producers working with free/open-source audio plug-ins?**

Technology is so amazing in this time! There are so many good music creation/production tools out there for free that it is completely possible to make music without ever having to pirate *or* pay for software. You don't have to pay thousands for software or studio time to make good, legitimate music. All you need are some good ideas, a mind open to possibilities, and the need to create!

# Index